CW00484750

Compliance, Codes and Communications

A practical guide to pharmaceutical marketing in the UK

Sixth edition: Covering the 2019 ABPI Code

Dr Judith Grice

This book is dedicated to
Chris

Published by Stanford Publishing Limited
in association with
PharmaCodes Compliance Limited www.pharmacodes.com

© 2019 Stanford Publishing Limited
www.stanfordpublishing.co.uk

All rights reserved. No part of this publication may be reproduced, stored in a retrieval system or transmitted in any form or by any means, electronic, mechanical, photocopying, recording or otherwise, except as permitted by the UK Copyright, Designs and Patents Act 1988, without prior permission in writing from the publishers.

Whilst the advice and information contained in this book are believed to be true and accurate, the authors, publisher and PharmaCodes Compliance Ltd make no representation, express or implied, with regard to the accuracy of the information contained in this book and cannot accept any legal responsibility or liability for any errors or omissions that may be made.

First published 2009
Second edition 2010
Third edition 2014
Fourth edition 2015
Fifth edition 2016
This edition published 2019
ISBN 978-0-9934073-2-1

A catalogue record for this title is available from the British Library.

Layout by 2m Partnership Limited www.2m.org.uk
Printed in the United Kingdom by Cambrian Printers www.cambrian-printers.co.uk

Contents

Introduction

This book has been fully revised to take account of the recent changes to the Association of British Pharmaceutical Industry (ABPI) Code[1] which became effective on 1 January 2019.

There is a transitional period before becoming fully operative on 1st May 2019. During the period 1st January 2019 and 30th April 2019, no promotional material or activity will be regarded as being in breach of the Code if it fails to comply with its provisions only because of newly-introduced requirements.

The changes to the last few editions of the Code have been minor compared with those prior to 2015 and the changes to the 2016 Code are no exception to this trend. Many are as a result of the PMCPA wishing to simplify the Code making requirements clearer to companies. One of the main changes is to Clause 14, allowing appropriately qualified persons to certify meetings and printed materials under clearly defined specific circumstances. Refer to **Basic Principles** page 3.

How to use this book

Chapter 1 is a concise review of the 'Basic Principles and Procedures' of the Code and this is the only section that I would advise anyone new to the ABPI Code to read and become familiar with, as these principles are applicable to most, if not all, promotional and non-promotional activities.

The subsequent chapters are intended to be dipped in and out of as a quick reference guide when starting to plan promotional or non-promotional activities and when practical advice is required for specific circumstances.

The chapters in general are structured to provide the following:
- ▶ Easy-to-understand information on the Code of Practice. This is often presented in tabular summaries so the requirements can be rapidly understood;
- ▶ Suggestions on how to interpret the rules for a wide range of activities;
- ▶ 'Hints and tips' on how to stay compliant. These are provided in call-out boxes to illustrate key points;
- ▶ 'Case reports', where available, providing important insights into interpretation of

the Code. The codes of practice are similar in many ways to the law, in that the interpretation is tested by case law. With new areas of the Code this testing is still to take place.

Limitations of this book

It is important that the limitations of this book are understood:

- ▶ It is **NOT** intended to replace reading or referring to the ABPI Code; it is intended as a companion to the Code. Every attempt has been made to ensure accuracy but any interpretations and summaries are either my opinion or those of Paul Woods, who co-authored some of the earlier editions. Therefore, you should always read the applicable codes, regulations or relevant guidance (e.g. the MHRA Blue Guide[3]) and where there are any discrepancies between these texts and this book, the texts should be followed;

- ▶ This book is **NOT** intended to be a totally comprehensive analysis of all possible challenges to promotional and communications materials and activities. It is based on the scope of the ABPI code and I have made reference to UK pharmaceutical marketing regulations where these are particularly important. However, legal action is also possible from other directions (e.g. competition law) and from other countries (for some companies the US legislation will be very important). Experts in these areas should be consulted when relevant;

- ▶ This book is **NOT** intended to replace asking colleagues for help and advice. With this in mind, I should like to thank Paul Woods for his valuable contributions and the benefit of his experience in the first two editions of this book. He was the original author for Chapters 4 and 5.

Judith Grice

CHAPTER 1

Basic Principles

Index of basic principles and procedures

The basic principles of the Code apply to many different forms of promotion and promotional activities directed towards UK healthcare professionals (HCPs) and other relevant decision makers. For example, wherever a claim is made for a product, whether it is in an electronic or printed advertisement or detail aid used by a sales representative or a booth panel, then it must be capable of substantiation.

Therefore the following section of basic principles and procedures will be referred to throughout the different sections of the book.

N.B. This chapter and indeed all of this book is intended as a companion to, and not a replacement for, the ABPI 2019 Code.

Adverse events

It is extremely important that any claims that are made regarding the safety and side effects of a product are accurate and reflect the available evidence. In general the following rules should be adhered to:

▶ The word 'safe' must never be used to describe a medicinal product without proper qualification;

▶ It must not be stated that a product has no side effects, toxic hazards or risks of addiction or dependency.

Mandatory wording Clause 4.9, 23.3

It is a requirement in the UK that all promotional material includes prominent (i.e. font larger than font used for prescribing information) mandatory wording. Wording should be as follows: *"Adverse events should be reported. Reporting forms and information can be found at [a web address which links directly to the MHRA yellow card site]. Adverse events should also be reported to [name of relevant pharmaceutical company]"*. A telephone number or e-mail address for the relevant department within the company may be included. When the website address is changed by the MHRA companies must use the new address within one year of the change.

Patient materials

Any material relating to a medicine intended for patients taking it must include the statement below or a similar one which conveys the same meaning:

> "*Reporting of side effects*
> *If you get any side effects, talk to your doctor, pharmacist or nurse. This includes any possible side effects not listed in the package leaflet. You can also report side effects directly via the Yellow Card Scheme at [www.mhra.gov.uk/yellowcard]. By reporting side effects you can help provide more information on the safety of this medicine.*"

When the material relates to a medicine which is subject to additional monitoring an inverted black equilateral triangle must be included on it together with the statement below or a similar one: '*This medicine is subject to additional monitoring. This will allow quick identification of new safety information. You can help by reporting any side effects you may get. See www.mhra.gov.uk/yellowcard for how to report side effects.*'

Black triangle   Clause 4.10

Promotional material must show an inverted black equilateral triangle when required by the licensing authorities (usually for new products). It means that additional monitoring of adverse events is required. The size of the black triangle depends on the size of the promotional item: for A4 size, each side of the triangle needs to be 5mm; for A5 it should be 3mm; and for A3, 7.5mm. In abbreviated adverts larger than A5 (but not larger than 420cm^2) each side of the black triangle should be no less than 5mm. The triangle needs to appear once and be located adjacent to the most prominent display of the name of the product.

In digital communications, the black triangle must be located adjacent to the first mention of the product and be of a sufficient size to be easily readable.

European pharmacovigilance legislation now requires the black triangle and wording which explains its meaning to appear on Summary of Product Characteristics (SPCs) and package leaflets (these documents are not classed as promotional materials). The size of the black triangle in these documents has to be proportionate to the font size of the text but must be a minimum of 5mm per side.

N.B. These requirements do not apply to promotional materials. If the materials are intended for use by patients, note the requirements listed under **Mandatory Wording – Patient Materials** above.

Artwork   Clause 7

Artwork must be acceptable in terms of the impression that it creates and must not be likely to cause offence or be misleading. It must be consistent with the SPC. For example, if a product is not licensed in children under 2 years of age, a child who appears to be younger than this should not be used in the artwork even if the child is actually older than the minimum age quoted in the SPC. It is the impression given that is important and if there are significant indication restrictions the advertisement text should make this clear. Similarly if a product is contraindicated in those who drive or operate machinery, using a tractor driver, forklift truck driver or other machine operative in the artwork advertising the product would be unacceptable as it may mislead the reader to think that the product could be safely used in these types of patient. Therefore it is important to consider:

▶ The licensed age groups;

▶ Any particular precautions or contraindications;

▶ The images, could they cause offence, e.g. for cultural or religious reasons, or be misleading.

Certification and examination   Clause 14

Companies must have a procedure to certify the following:

▶ All promotional materials (including meeting materials), relevant representative briefing materials and promotional aids;

▶ All documents and arrangements for meetings which involve travel outside the UK (Refer to **Meetings** for the exceptions), including:
   - Programme
   - Venue and reasons for using that venue
   - Intended audience
   - Anticipated cost
   - Details of hospitality;

▶ Non-promotional materials which relate to medicines and diseases such as:
   - Educational materials for the public or patients
   - Material relating to medical and educational goods and services (including internal company instructions)
   - Material relating to working with patient organisations, NHS joint working, patient support programme materials.

The materials should be in their final form and no amendments made after the certification. The signatory is certifying that in their opinion the material is:

▶ In accordance with the requirements of the relevant advertising regulations;

▶ Complies with the ABPI Code;

▶ Is not inconsistent with the marketing authorisation and the summary of product characteristics;

▶ Is a fair and truthful presentation of the facts about the medicine.

The approval certificates can be either paper or electronic but must be retained for a minimum of 3 years. Any materials still in use after two years must be recertified.

Nominated signatories

Materials and activities requiring certification must be certified by a nominated signatory who must be a registered medical practitioner or a pharmacist registered in the UK, or alternatively, in the case of a product for dental use only, a UK-registered dentist. The nominated signatory certifying the materials must not be responsible for developing or drawing them up.

The only exceptions to the requirement for the signatory to be a registered medical practitioner or uk registered pharmacist are meetings and printed materials in certain specific circumstances as described below:

Meetings

Meetings which involve travel outside the UK still require certification in advance but this can be carried out by an appropriately qualified person. However they must still have relevant experience, a detailed knowledge of the Code and be of sufficient length of service and seniority to undertake this important task.

Meetings involving travel outside the UK do not require either certification or examination if the company's only involvement is to support a speaker to present at the meeting and there is no pharmaceutical company involvement with the meeting at all e.g. a learned society meeting.

Additionally, if an overseas company arranges for a UK speaker to present at a meeting to be held outside the UK the presentation materials do not need to be certified or examined by the UK company provided there are no UK delegates and the UK company has no role in arranging the meeting or the presentation.

Printed materials

When the final form is a printed item, the final electronic version must be certified by one of the medical signatories. However the printed version may be certified by an appropriately qualified person i.e. anyone the company considers appropriately qualified such as a proof reader, medical information etc. In these circumstances the material will have two certificates both of which must be retained.

Notification of signatories

The names and qualifications of the company's nominated signatories must be notified (in advance) to the advertising standards unit vigilance and risk management of medicines division of the Medicines and Healthcare products Regulatory Agency (MHRA) and to the Prescription Medicines Code of Practice Authority (PMCPA). The MHRA and PMCPA must also be provided with these details for any designated alternative signatories. They must be promptly notified about any changes to these names.

When companies co-promote products or work together in other ways, e.g. joint working projects, they may decide to have only one final signatory to certify on behalf of all the companies. The PMCPA and MHRA must be notified in advance of this arrangement including the names of all signatories. However if a complaint is made, each company involved in the project/activity is held responsible.

Non-promotional items

Other non-promotional items do not require formal certification but should be examined for compliance with the Code and regulations. In practice most companies use the same or similar procedures for examination to ensure accuracy and compliance. These items include:

- ▶ Corporate advertising;
- ▶ Press releases;
- ▶ Market research materials;
- ▶ Financial information to inform shareholders and the Stock Exchange;
- ▶ Medical information letters written in response to unsolicited questions from the public, etc.;
- ▶ Non-interventional studies.

Finally, as mentioned above, although it is only meetings which involve travel outside the UK which require formal certification or examination, the Code states that companies must ensure that all meetings are checked to see that they comply with the Code. Companies are required to have written policies and procedures on meetings and hospitality and the associated allowable expenditure. However these procedures in many companies require the certification of all meetings.

Company commissioned articles and papers `Clause 9.10`

Materials commissioned by pharmaceutical companies must clearly indicate the name of the company and the sponsorship even if they are not promotional. This includes information relating to human health or diseases which is sponsored by a pharmaceutical company.

However, it does not normally include market research material, which need not reveal the name of the company involved but must make it clear that a pharmaceutical company (not necessarily named) sponsored the research.

Comparison and hanging comparatives `Clause 7`

Statements in promotional materials that compare one product with another product must be:

- ▶ Accurate and balanced;
- ▶ Fair and objective;
- ▶ Up to date;
- ▶ Not misleading (refer to **Exaggerated, false or misleading claims**) or disparaging; and
- ▶ Capable of substantiation (refer to **Substantiation**).

In addition to the above, comparisons can only be made between medicines and services intended for the same needs or purpose.

If a statement comparing a product to a competitor product is not consistent with the UK SPC of the competitor then this must not lead to an unfair comparison or be misleading. The statement must clearly indicate that it is not consistent with the competitor SPC. It should also not promote that product for an unlicensed use because under EU law you do not have to be the licence holder to be subject to the requirements of the advertising legislation.

The brand names of a competitor products may be used in promotional materials provided that:

▶ The competitors' brand name is not disparaged, discredited or denigrated in any way;
▶ Unfair advantage is not taken of the reputation of a competitor's trade mark, brand name or branding;
▶ Your product or service is not presented as an imitation or replica of a competitor product or service.
▶ There is no confusion created between your product and those of competitors;
▶ Trademarks should be properly distinguished and acknowledged, e.g. 'Product X' is a trademark belonging to 'Company Y'.

Safety comparisons can be made provided they comply with the above requirements but must never imply that a competitor product is unsafe.

Hanging comparatives should not be used when promoting medicines in the UK. A hanging comparative is where, for example, product X is said to be better, faster, cheaper, etc. without saying compared to what. The example often used is of the soap powder brand name Persil where the statement used is 'Persil washes whiter'. This is a hanging comparative, as the statement does not explain what Persil washes whiter than. If Persil were a medicine this statement would not be allowed in promotional materials. 'Persil washes whiter than Brand X' may be allowed if this claim could be verified.

If the claim is not qualified further the following are examples of hanging comparatives:

▶ Increased response;
▶ Decreased response;
▶ More effective;
▶ Better tolerability; and
▶ Stronger.

Compassionate use `Clause 3`

Some companies provide medicine on a compassionate use basis to patients who are suffering from a disease for which no satisfactory authorised alternative therapy exists or who cannot enter a clinical trial. The supply of the product must be carried out in line with regulations for such a supply but the product is unlicensed and may not be promoted.

Conditional marketing authorisation `Clause 3`

Medicines that address unmet medical needs of patients are sometimes granted a conditional licence on the basis of less comprehensive data than is normally required. The available data must indicate that the medicine's benefits outweigh its risks and the applicant will usually be required to provide the comprehensive clinical data in the future.

If a medicine is granted a conditional licence this meets the requirements of clause 1.3 of the Code and it can be legitimately promoted within the terms of this conditional licence. Wherever possible relevant information should be added to national horizon scanning databases.

Consistency with the marketing authorisation `Clause 3`

It is a requirement of the ABPI Code and the advertising regulations that promotion must be in accordance with the terms of its marketing authorisation and must not be inconsistent with the summary of product characteristics (SPC).

However this does not mean that only information contained within the SPC can be used to promote the product. It just means that promotional copy must not contradict the SPC and must be consistent with ALL sections of the SPC. The following are some examples.

Dose
Promotion must be consistent with the dose, dosing frequency and any length of treatment contained in the SPC. If, for example, the licensed dose is 'one capsule daily for 7 days', it is not permissible to promote doses of 'one capsule twice a day', or treatment periods longer or shorter than 7 days. Promotion could be taken to include the use of statements from, or referencing studies, that use unlicensed doses. It is permissible in some instances to reference such a study, for example with respect to some aspect that was not dose related, providing the unlicensed use is not promoted.

Indications
A product may only be promoted for the indications for which it is licensed. For example product X is only licensed for the treatment of heart failure in patients categorised New York Heart Association (NYHA) classes I to III when product A has proved unsuitable. It must be clear in any promotion that product X:
> ▶ Is licensed to be used second line after product A has been unsuccessfully used;
> ▶ Is not licensed to be used in NYHA class IV.

The consequences of using a treatment cannot be promoted unless they are also contained within the licence. For example antihypertensives cannot be promoted for reduction of death from myocardial infarction or stroke (even though it may be generally accepted to be true) unless this is also a licensed indication.

Patient population, contraindications and warnings
A product should not be promoted for a patient group that is not within its licence, for example:
> ▶ Children;
> ▶ The elderly; or
> ▶ Those with concomitant diseases which are contraindicated such as hepatic or renal disease.

Efficacy

It is often the case that pivotal studies are extended to provide longer term efficacy data than was available at the time of the licence submission and therefore contained within the SPC. It is permissible to use these data in promotion provided the SPC does not state information to the contrary, e.g. 'Product X has consistently maintained efficacy for 5 years' would NOT be acceptable if the SPC for product X states either 'efficacy beyond 3 years has not been established' or 'it is recommended that the product only be used for 24 months...'

Adverse events

When the words 'Very Common', 'Common', 'Uncommon', 'Rare' and 'Very Rare' are used in advertising and promotion, the meaning of them must be the same as the SPC. For example, if you state that a type of adverse event is 'Rare' it must have an occurrence of between 1 in 1000 and 1 in 10,000. SPCs usually use the following terms defined in the way shown:

- Very common (> 1/10);
- Common (>1/100, <1/10);
- Uncommon (>1/1,000, <1/100);
- Rare (>1/10,000, <1/1,000);
- Very rare (<1/10,000).

It shouldn't be claimed that a product 'has an excellent safety profile' or is 'well tolerated' if this isn't consistent with the adverse event profile listed in the SPC.

Consultancy agreements and payments Clause 23

Healthcare professionals can be engaged by pharmaceutical companies to provide a variety of services for example speaking at meetings, participating in advisory board meetings, assisting with training or as investigators in clinical trial programmes.

Whenever external consultants are engaged, a written consultancy agreement must be drawn up in advance of the commencement of the services and a record of it must be kept. The consultancy agreement is detailed in Clause 23 and must fulfil the following criteria:

- The service to be provided and the basis for payment of fees;
- The legitimate and identified need for the services;
- The selection of consultant must be by a person with appropriate expertise;
- The number of consultants engaged must not be more than reasonably necessary to achieve the identified need;
- Payments to consultants must be appropriate and represent a fair market value for the services provided. BMA guidelines lay down rates for certain services and these can be used as a benchmark to calculate appropriate levels of payment for services provided to companies;
- The company must include in contracts a requirement that the consultant declares their consultancy when writing or speaking in public on any relevant topic. Similarly if a company employs a practising HCP on a part-time basis, they must

ensure that the HCP declares this employment whenever they write or speak on a subject connected to the employment or the company employing them.

▶ Companies must have arrangements in place so that ToV are disclosed in compliance with data privacy requirements. Consultants must be aware of this disclosure process.

The contracting company must make appropriate use of the services of the consultant and hiring the consultant to provide the service must not be an inducement.

Disclosure of payments

Pharmaceutical companies must publicly disclose details of the fees paid to UK HCPs engaged as consultants (or to employers on their behalf) for their services. These should be declared at an individual level if the HCP gives their consent. However, if consent is withheld for any item, the total amount of fees paid may be disclosed as an aggregated amount. Fees and related expenses (agreed in the fees for service or consultancy contract) must both be disclosed separately.

Disclosure should be made annually in respect of each calendar year and must be in the first six months after the end of the calendar year in which the transfers were made, i.e. in 2019 for transfers of value made in 2018. Further information is available in **Table 1: Summary of requirements when disclosing transfers of value to HCPs and HCOs.** This information must remain in the public domain for at least 3 years but companies must retain their records for at least 5 years after the end of the calendar year in which the payments were made.

Disclosure must be made on a central platform. The template which is to be used is available to download from the Authority's website (**www.pmcpa.org.uk**).

The requirements concerning disclosure of payments to consultants also include payments for research and development work, including the conduct of clinical trials. Further information is available in **Table 1: Summary of requirements when disclosing transfers of value to HCPs and HCOs** in the clinical research section.

Date of promotional material Clause 4.8

Promotional materials (other than those appearing as an integral part of a professional publication and those exempt from obligatory requirements, see **Obligatory information**) must

---

Learning from a Case: Auth/2724/7/14 – Cost comparison
This complaint concerned a cost comparison chart where two different doses of the company's product (one of which was used infrequently and not specifically listed in the SPC) were included in a comparison with the SPC doses of competitors. The Panel ruled that as equal weight had been given to both doses in the comparison that this was not comparing like with like and therefore misleading and a breach of clause 7.2 was ruled.
Learning Point:
• Great care must be taken when making cost comparisons that 'like is being compared with like'.

include the date that the promotional item was drawn up or last revised. **N.B.** This is in addition to the requirements that the date the prescribing information (PI) was last drawn up or revised is included in the PI (see **Obligatory information**). This often means that promotional materials bear two different dates.

Disguised promotion `Clause 12`

Promotion must not be disguised as non-promotional activity. Examples of activities that could be ruled as disguised promotion if not conducted appropriately include:

► Clinical assessments;
► Medical information letters;
► Post-marketing surveillance and experience programmes;
► Post-authorisation studies; and
► Market research.

Such assessments, programmes and studies must be conducted with a primarily scientific or educational purpose. Promotion must not involve disparaging reports regarding the clinical and scientific opinions of health professionals and must be ethical at all times.

Disparaging reports and claims `Clause 8.1 and 8.2`

Promotion must not involve disparaging copy or reports regarding the clinical and scientific opinions of health professionals. The medicines, products and activities of other pharmaceutical companies must not be disparaged.

Early access to medicines scheme `Clause 3`

This is a scheme designed to give patients access to medicines before the full process to grant a marketing authorisation or licence extension for additional indications has been completed. This means that patients may gain access to a medicine up to 2 years earlier than would have otherwise been possible. However medicines with early access approval are not licensed and therefore must not be promoted. Wherever possible relevant information must added to horizon scanning databases.

Economic evaluations `Clause 7.2`

Comparisons of the costs of products can be made at different levels of complexity ranging from simple cost comparisons to complex economic evaluations involving quality of life assessments. As with any claim it is important that the basis for any comparison is accurate, fair, balanced, not misleading or exaggerated and up-to-date. Any assumptions made in economic evaluations must be clinically appropriate and consistent with the product's Marketing Authorisation (MA).

The basis for selection of comparators should be made clear and in order for cost comparisons to be fair it is important to compare 'like with like', e.g. cost per tablet or per ml, cost per day or per treatment course. However even these comparisons may not be fair under certain circumstances:

- ▶ Cost per tablet would not be fair if the number of tablets required for a course of treatment is different for the comparators;
- ▶ Cost per day would not be fair if the length of the course of treatments differs for the comparators;
- ▶ Cost per ml would not be fair if the volume per dose varies between the comparators.

In addition to being fair comparisons, the basis for selection must be valid, for example all the products in the same therapeutic class. It would not be considered fair to choose only the most expensive product in the therapeutic class to use as a comparator.

The following list, although not comprehensive, contains those comparisons that are commonly used in promotional materials:
- ▶ Simple cost comparison;
- ▶ Cost effectiveness;
- ▶ Cost benefit;
- ▶ Cost utility.

Simple cost comparison[4]

This is an analysis of the comparative costs of alternative interventions or programmes. It does not include consequences.

Cost effectiveness analysis (CEA)[5]

An economic evaluation in which the costs and consequences of alternative interventions are expressed in cost per unit of health outcome. CEA is used to determine technical efficiency, i.e. comparison of costs and consequences of competing interventions for a given patient group within a given budget.

Cost benefit analysis (CBA)[5]

This is an economic evaluation in which all costs and consequences of a programme are expressed in the same units, usually money. CBA is used to determine allocative efficiency, i.e. comparison of costs and benefits across programmes serving different patient groups. N.B. Even if some items of resource or benefit cannot be measured in the common unit of account (e.g. money) they should not be excluded from the analysis.

Cost utility analysis (CUA)[5]

This is a form of economic study design in which interventions that produce different consequences, in terms of both quantity and quality of life, are expressed as 'utilities'. These are measures which comprise both length of life and subjective levels of well-being. The best known utility measure is the 'quality adjusted life year' or QALY. In this case, competing interventions are compared in terms of cost per utility (cost per QALY).

Exaggerated, false or misleading claims Clause 7.2, 7.8 and 7.10

It is important that claims made for medicines do not mislead either intentionally or unintentionally. Therefore it is important to consider whether the information presented in

Learning from a Case: Auth/2757/5/15 – Data from models and simulations
This case concerned the use of data derived from simulations or 'models' alongside actual clinical data in a promotional presentation. The Panel noted that the slide in question, containing simulated data, was presented between two other slides which contained actual clinical data. They ruled that this was misleading as it was not made clear that the data was simulated.
Learning Point:
- If using non-clinical data such as a pharmacokinetic simulations make sure that this is very clearly stated.

advertising and promotion can be misconstrued in any way. The ways that graphs are presented and statistics are used in promotional items are common causes of false or misleading claims. Graphs will therefore be looked at in more detail:

Graphs

The main principle behind the ABPI Code is that data are presented in a clear, accurate way so as not to mislead the reader.

DO

> ▶ Label axes of graphs with parameter and unit of measurement;
> ▶ Ensure adequate and accurate referencing;
> ▶ Include statistical information and ensure that this is accurately presented, e.g. p values where relevant, or stating 'not statistically significant' if the data presented do not have statistical significance;
> ▶ Include all relevant data, e.g. patient numbers; and
> ▶ Make it clear if the data presented are from different studies. It is misleading to present data from two or more studies in one graph as though it were all from the same study. This is because there will be differences, for example in study protocols, patient demographics and numbers. It would also be misleading, even if the multiple origins are made clear, unless the studies are truly identical in all significant respects.

DO NOT

> ▶ Use suppressed zeros when the aim is to convey the message that Drug X gives better results than Drug Y. The difference between the two is accentuated by shortening the axis. This is illustrated in Figure 1: Drug X gives increased response compared to Y and it can be seen in Figure 2, where the X-axis starts at 60% response (i.e. a suppressed zero), that the difference between the drugs looks much greater than the difference in Figure 1 where the axis starts at zero. However suppressed zeros are not considered misleading and may be used if the message is that two products are similar, providing that, in all cases statistical significance (or lack of it) is clearly stated;
> ▶ Extrapolate the graph into an area where there are no data;
> ▶ Select only part of the data for use in a graph if this gives a misleading impression. This is illustrated both in Figures 3 and 4: Increase in blood cell count Drug A compared to Drug B and Figure 5: Percentage decrease in symptoms Drug C compared to Drug D.

Learning from a Case: Auth/2726/8/14 – Presenting data in context

This case concerned the use of secondary endpoint data from a large study where the primary endpoint had failed to reach statistical significance. The panel found that the secondary data had been presented inconsistently across several different promotional pieces and in several instances the secondary endpoint had not been presented in the context of the failed primary endpoint. This is misleading and a breach of clauses 7.2, 7.4 & 9.1 was ruled.

Learning Point:

- If presenting data on secondary endpoints where the primary has not met statistical significance, a clear statement to that effect must appear before the secondary data is presented. Ensure this is done consistently on all promotional material and on each slide/piece where the secondary data is presented.

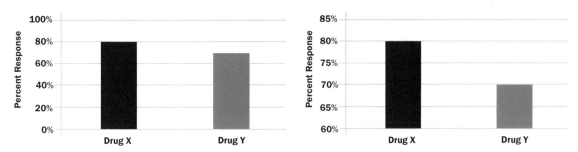

Figure 1: Drug X gives increased response compared to Drug Y

Figure 2: Drug X gives increased response compared to Drug Y

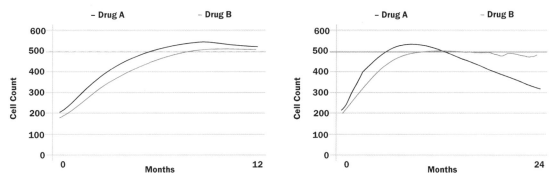

Figure 3: Increase in blood cell count Drug A compared to Drug B after 12 months

Figure 4: Increase in blood cell count Drug A compared to Drug B after 24 months

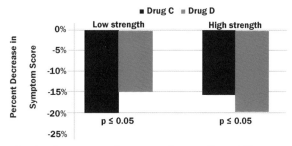

Figure 5: Percentage decrease in symptoms Drug C compared to Drug D

Another important consideration is that the Code requires that if a graph is taken from a published study it must be 'faithfully reproduced'. Modification is allowed if needed to comply with the Code (e.g. to eliminate a suppressed zero) but it must be clearly stated that the material has been modified.

With regard to the data illustrated in Figures 3 and 4, the pharmaceutical company marketing Drug A would be misleading if they used the 12-month data alone if the 24-month data were known. In Figure 5, if the data for just the low strength of the two drugs were used promotionally by the pharmaceutical company marketing Drug C this may be misleading, as there is a better response at the higher dose for Drug D. However selective use of data would be justified, and often mandatory, if using the whole of the data is outside the terms of the product licence. For example, it would be justified to omit the data for strengths of product that are not licensed.

Risk reductions

Referring to the benefits of a medicine by quoting a risk reduction without mentioning absolute risk may make a product appear more effective than it is. Therefore relative risk may only be used when absolute risk is also quoted. However absolute risk may be quoted without referring to relative risk.

Absolute risk: The absolute risk of a disease is the risk of developing a particular disease over a time period.

Relative risk: This is used to compare the risk in two different groups of people.

Example: Women have a 4 in 50 chance of developing a particular disease by the time they reach 65. Research shows that a new treatment reduces the relative risk of getting this disease by 50%. The 50% is the relative risk reduction and is referring to the 4, 50% of 4 is 2. This means that the absolute risk is reduced from 4 in 50 to 2 in 50.

Footnotes Clause 7

Footnotes are allowed to be used in promotional materials to provide additional information. For example, let's assume that Brand A is a prostaglandin licensed for the treatment of glaucoma and the body copy has the statement:

> 'Brand A has been shown to reduce intraocular pressure to less than 16mmHg in
> 95% of glaucoma patients *'

then if the related footnote read:

> '*In a randomised double blind placebo-controlled study involving 300 patients'

then this will be permissible as it gives the reader more information about the study.

They **SHOULD NOT** be used to correct claims. You should assume that the healthcare professional may not see the footnote, and the large font 'strapline' read alone should not mislead the reader into believing that the drug is more effective or has a more favourable tolerability profile than it has been shown to have in clinical studies.

So if the footnote in the above example read:

'*When used in conjunction with a beta-blocker'

this would be clearly an attempt to mislead the reader by making an exaggerated claim and attempting to qualify the claim with the footnote. This is **UNACCEPTABLE**.

Good taste and suitability Clause 9

Promotion should be carried out in such a way that it recognises the special nature of medicines; they must not be promoted as if they are general commodities.

▶ Companies must maintain high ethical standards at all times and recognise the professional standing of the recipients. Unprofessional styles of promotion, e.g. the use of gimmicks, over-simplistic advertising and tasteless ostentatious advertising must be avoided. It is also important to avoid extremes of format, size or cost of promotional material.

▶ Promotion must not cause offence.

– Sexual imagery must not be used to attract attention to materials

– This can be a difficult area as the subjects and images that may cause offence vary around the world and in different religious and cultural groups. This should be remembered when producing materials for use at international congresses as well as routinely in the UK with its multicultural society.

– The use of inappropriate language and abbreviations or emoticons should be avoided particularly in digital communications.

– Caution should be exercised when using humour in promotional materials because it may be received very differently by different people.

– Names or photographs of HCPs must not be used in way that differs from the principles or standards of that profession.

▶ Teaser adverts, which raise interest in *something* without providing any information as to what that *something* is, e.g. 'coming soon', are unacceptable.

▶ The provision of private prescription pads pre-printed with the name of a medicine is unacceptable.

▶ Reproductions of official documents must not be used promotionally unless appropriate written permission is obtained.

Health professional Clause 1.4

The term 'health professional' or 'healthcare professional' (HCP) includes members of the medical, dental, pharmacy and nursing professions and any other persons who in the course of their professional activities may administer, prescribe, purchase, recommend or supply a medicine.

Imitation of competitor products/trade names Clause 7.3

Companies should not imitate the promotion of competitors in a way that is likely to mislead or confuse, for example by using devices, copy, slogans or general layout that has been adopted by other companies and is likely to be associated with that company. The medicines, products and activities of other pharmaceutical companies must not be disparaged.

MHRA pre-vetting of promotional materials

The MHRA pre-vets promotional materials for new active substances and those where there have been serious breaches of the regulations.

The period of vetting will normally be one to three months and not normally for longer than six months. This time period may be reduced or extended depending on the quality of the initial advertising material submitted and the time period over which materials are received. Promotional material submitted for vetting to the MHRA should indicate the target audience and include references in support of claims in the promotional material. The MHRA also expects non-promotional items, such as press releases and risk minimisation plans and materials, to be submitted for review to ensure that these are not promotional. All materials to be vetted should have already undergone a full set of internal quality control and compliance checks before submission to the MHRA.

The MHRA will undertake to give its opinion on the advertising material normally within five working days but where substantial data are submitted this will not be possible and the MHRA will give an estimate of the time necessary to complete the assessment. The company should keep the MHRA informed of when they are likely to submit advertising for review.

New `Clause 7.11`

In the UK 'New' must only be used in promotional materials when referring to a product, or presentation which has been generally available or any therapeutic indication which has been promoted for 12 months.

Non-proprietary name `Clause 4.3`

The non-proprietary name, or list of active ingredients (using approved names if they exist), must appear immediately before, immediately after, immediately above or immediately below the most prominent display of the brand name in BOLD type font lower case 'x' is no less than 2mm in height or type size so they occupy no less total area than that taken up by the brand name. Clause 4.3 does not require the brand name to be included, only the non-proprietary name; however in practice both are included. In electronic advertisements the non-proprietary name or list of approved ingredients must appear adjacent to the first appearance of the brand name in such a size that the information is readily readable.

Obligatory information `Clause 4`

The following are required to appear on all promotional items. There are specific exemptions, e.g. abbreviated advertisements and booth panels (refer to **Chapter 3: Printed Materials**).
- ▶ Prescribing information (refer to **Prescribing information**);
- ▶ Non-proprietary name or list of approved ingredients (refer to **Non-proprietary name**);
- ▶ Reference number (refer to **Reference number**);
- ▶ Black triangle - if required (refer to **Black triangle**);

- ► Adverse event mandatory wording (refer to **Adverse events**);
- ► Date of promotional material (refer to **Date**).

Prescribing information `Clause 4.2`

The requirement to provide prescribing information on promotional materials can be fulfilled by including the following on the materials:
- ► The cost (excluding VAT) where needed; and
- ► The legal classification of the product.

Plus either the SPC **or** the abbreviated prescribing information.

If the abbreviated PI is used **in addition to the cost and legal classification of the product** it must consist of the following:
- ► The product name, either brand or generic;
- ► A list of active ingredients and quantity of each, using approved names or international non-proprietary names (INN);
- ► One or more licensed indication(s);
- ► The recommended dosage and method of use;
- ► Any warnings issued by the regulators;
- ► A list of both common and serious side effects with a statement that prescribers should consult the SPC in relation to other side effects;
- ► The name and address of the marketing authorisation (MA) holder or business responsible for sale and supply;
- ► The product licence number;
- ► The date the PI was drawn up or last revised (this is in addition to the date of the promotional item itself).

Prescribing information must:
- ► Be positioned so it can easily be read, i.e. the reader shouldn't need to turn the piece around;
- ► Form an integral part of the piece. Each promotional item must be able to stand alone. For example, if a mailing contains a detail aid, a bookmark and a letter, all three items must include the PI;
- ► In the case of abbreviated prescribing information (API) it must include information from the SPC that is directly relevant to the promotional piece concerned, e.g. indications and dosage data must relate directly to the promotional messages in the piece.

N.B. In the case of electronic advertisements it is possible to provide the SPC part of the above requirements by providing a link to it. However including a web address on printed materials is not acceptable.

For more information regarding exact requirements for specific printed or electronic materials, refer to **Chapter 3: Printed Materials** and **Chapter 7: Digital Media**.

Pre-licence period `Clause 3`

Medicines cannot be promoted prior to the granting of the marketing authorisation (licence). Sales representatives are by the very nature of their role involved in promoting medicines, and should not be involved in the pre-licensing period to communicate to HCPs information about unlicensed products or off-label indications. However certain activities are acceptable and some, such as notifying the budget holders, are even encouraged in the pre-licensing period. Examples include:

- ▶ Corporate activity;
- ▶ Public relations;
- ▶ Medical information;
- ▶ Scientific exchange of information;
- ▶ Notification to budget holders, e.g. health authorities.

Corporate activity

This may be either:

- ▶ Corporate advertising. A company may mention their interest in research and development in a specific therapeutic area in advertisements but they must not mention specific products by name or by implication. Further information is available in **Chapter 4: Public Relations**
- ▶ Financial information released in company annual reports or other financial information divulged to members of the business community such as financial analysts. This information must be accurate, balanced and the business purpose must be clear. Further information is available in **Chapter 4: Public Relations**.

Although these types of material do not require certification, because they are not promotional materials, they should be examined to ensure that they have not entered the promotional arena.

Public relations

This is covered in detail in **Chapter 4: Public Relations**.

Medical information

Medical information officers are allowed to respond to any **unsolicited** requests for information from healthcare professionals regarding the use of medicines. These can be:

- ▶ Within the terms of the licence;
- ▶ Off-label (licensed medicines outside of the terms of the licence);
- ▶ Medicines that do not have a licence.

However, the keyword is **unsolicited** which means it must not be prompted in any way. The following are examples that are **not acceptable**:

- ▶ Sales representatives prompting the request by suggesting that an HCP contacts medical information, e.g. by highlighting an unlicensed or off-label use by mentioning or showing a clinical paper;
- ▶ Materials distributed that suggest the reader may request further information, e.g. reply paid cards (if this information is unlicensed or off-label);

▶ Discussions at the commercial section of a booth which prompt a request for unlicensed or off-label information.

Scientific exchange of information

The legitimate exchange of medical and scientific information is allowed during the development of a medicine. This exchange of information may occur in a variety of ways:

▶ During non-promotional meetings, e.g. advisory boards and investigator meetings see **Chapter 2: Meetings**;

▶ Symposia at international congresses see **Chapter 2: Meetings**;

▶ Publications of clinical studies in medical and scientific journals.

The key point to note is that these activities must be carried out in a non-promotional manner without the use of branding.

Notification to budget holders

NHS organisations and others involved in the purchase of medicines need to estimate budgets in advance, so it is permissible to send information to them about unlicensed indications or products if these may have a significant impact on their expenditure including those that arise from changes in the patient pathway and/or service delivery. Notification can only be made to those who make policy decisions on budgets or are budget holders, e.g. health authorities, primary care organisations, hospital trusts but not prescribers. Companies wishing to provide advance notification must ensure that information is also provided, wherever possible, for inclusion in national horizon scanning databases.

The information provided must not be promotional in style, for example, no product logos, but company logos are allowed. Moderate use of the brand name of the product is permitted, but this must not be stylised. Mock ups or draft versions of either the summaries of product characteristics or package leaflets must not be used. The information must be factual and limited to that sufficient to provide an adequate but succinct account of the product's properties; other products should only be mentioned to put the new product into context in the therapeutic area concerned.

It should also state the following:

▶ Whether or not a new medicine or a change to an existing medicine is the subject of a marketing authorization in the UK;

▶ The likely cost or savings and budgetary implications (e.g. the need for service redesign) which must be such that they will significantly change the organisation's likely expenditure.

If requested, companies may provide further information or make a presentation about the product.

In order for information to be legitimately provided, the product should be one of the following:

▶ A new active substance; or

▶ Have a novel mode of delivery or administration; or

- ▶ A product which contains an active substance prepared in a new way, such as by the use of biotechnology; or
- ▶ A product which is to have a significant addition to the existing range of authorized indications.

Procedures `Guidelines page 53-59`

Companies must have written procedures to ensure that the following are carried out in an appropriate manner:

- ▶ Creation, review, approval and withdrawal of promotional materials;
- ▶ Training of sales representatives;
- ▶ Provision of medicines and samples;
- ▶ Meetings and hospitality;
- ▶ Relationships with patient organisations;
- ▶ Gifts, inducements, promotional aids and the provision of medical and educational goods and services;
- ▶ The internet;
- ▶ Non-interventional studies;
- ▶ Joint working between pharmaceutical companies and the NHS and others for the benefit of patients.

These are usually written in the form of Standard Operating Procedures (SOPs).

Promotion `Clause 1.2`

The Code covers a wide range of promotional and non-promotional activities undertaken by a pharmaceutical company. It is crucial to distinguish which activities are promotional and those which are not. This will depend not just on the item or activity itself but also on the purpose (actual and perceived), how the materials are used and the consequences of this use.

The Code defines 'promotion' as any activity undertaken by a pharmaceutical company or with its authority which promotes the administration, consumption, prescription, purchase, recommendation, sale, supply or use of its medicines.

The broad range of materials and activities which the Code considers to be "included" or "not included" in this definition are listed in Clause 1.2 of the ABPI 2019 Code.

> **Learning from a Case: Auth/2710/5/14 – Misleading promotion**
> A complaint was made about the phrase 'drug of choice' used in an advertisement when the licensed indication for the medicine was for use when other treatments were considered insufficient. The Panel ruled that even though the material had been reviewed by the MHRA, it still had to comply with the code. The claim implied that no other medicine could be chosen as a first line therapy, whereas the medicine was not licensed for first line use. A breach of clauses 7.2 & 7.4 was ruled.
> **Learning Points:**
> - Take care with all embracing claims such as 'drug of choice.'
> - MHRA review of the material does not negate compliance with the ABPI code.

Quotations `Clause 10`

Any quotations used:

- ▶ Must be capable of substantiation (refer to **Substantiation**);
- ▶ Must be accurate, fair and balanced;
- ▶ Must state the reference source;
- ▶ Must reflect the current views of the person quoted;
- ▶ Must, if unpublished, have the permission of the person quoted prior to use; and
- ▶ Must not be taken out of context.

Reference number `Guidelines page 54`

The 'guidelines on company procedures relating to the code of practice' recommend that each piece of promotional material should bear a unique reference number (one number per item) and that this should appear on the certificate approving the item for use. This is so that there can be no doubt as to what has been certified, and it is recommended that even if there are different sizes and layouts of an item, each should have its own unique reference number and individual certification. It is usual for this number to be allocated to the approval 'folder', this may be paper-based but it is more usual now for it to be electronic.

Relevant decision makers `Clause 1.5`

The term 'other relevant decision makers' particularly includes those with an NHS role who could influence in any way the administration, consumption, prescription, purchase, recommendation, sale, supply or use of any medicine but who are not health professionals.

Sanctions `Clause 2 and ABPI Constitution and Procedure`

Throughout this guidance there are examples of case reports that illustrate key learning from the cases brought before the PMCPA. The complaints' process is summarised in a schematic on page 43 and in detail on pages 45-52 of the ABPI 2019 Code. This guidance will not cover this in any detail but in summary, if a breach of a clause or clauses of the code is ruled after completion of the processes described in this schematic, an administrative fee may be charged to the offending company by the PMCPA. In addition the PMCPA may require the offending company to:

- ▶ Issue corrective statements;
- ▶ Recover promotional items;
- ▶ Undergo an audit of its processes and procedures.

In the most serious cases, a breach of Clause 2 may be ruled which means that the offending company has been found to bring discredit to, and a reduction of confidence in, the pharmaceutical industry. The ABPI Code gives examples of activities likely to be in breach of clause 2 as:

"prejudicing patient safety and/or public health, excessive hospitality, inducements to prescribe, unacceptable payments, inadequate action leading to a breach of undertaking, promotion prior to the grant of a marketing authorization, conduct of company employees/agents that falls short of competent care and multiple/ cumulative breaches of a similar and serious nature in the same therapeutic area within a short period of time".

On some occasions after such a finding, a company has been expelled from the ABPI, usually for a 3 or 6 month period.

Side effects `Clause 7.9`

It is extremely important that any claims that are made regarding the safety and side effects of a product are accurate and reflect the product licence and any available evidence. In general the following rules should be adhered to:

- ▶ The word 'safe' must never be used to describe a medicinal product without proper qualification;
- ▶ It must not be stated that a product has no side effects, toxic hazards or risks of addiction or dependency.

Substantiation `Clause 7.4 and 9.5`

Substantiation is the verification of claims or statements made in promotional materials. This verification is usually provided in promotional material by citing references. Promotional materials must not reference the Commission on Human Medicines, the Medicines Healthcare products Regulatory Agency (MHRA) or the licensing authority unless specifically required to do so by the licensing authority. In general terms, substantiation by referencing is required in promotion in the following circumstances:

- ▶ When a quotation is used;
- ▶ When a clinical trial is used; and
- ▶ When graphs, tables, figures and artwork are used.

When data from a clinical trial is used companies, must ensure (if necessary) that the trial and its results have been disclosed in accordance with clause 13.1. Requests for substantiation of approved indications may not be refused, but providing a copy of the SPC will satisfy the company's responsibility. Substantiation must be provided to healthcare professionals, including those working for competitors, if requested as soon as possible and certainly within 10 days. The type of data allowed to substantiate statements varies from country to country, but the UK allows all of the four following types of data:

- ▶ Published data, e.g. from journals in the public domain;
- ▶ Abstracts, e.g. from data presented at international conferences;
- ▶ Posters, e.g. presented at international conferences;
- ▶ Data on file. This is data that is not in the public domain, e.g. unpublished clinical studies from the pharmaceutical company making the claim.

However, it should be borne in mind that all these types of data may not be allowed to verify claims in other countries. This can be important if, for example, your company is exhibiting at an international congress and requirements of the national Code where the congress is taking place should be verified with the local signatory for the materials. The reason that some types of data are not allowed in certain countries is because of the quality of the different types of data. The perceived quality of the data and its credibility is highest for published data especially if the journal is peer reviewed. The credibility decreases moving down the list above.

When using data on file, the following factors should be taken into account:
- ▶ Only cite data you are prepared to provide. Care must be taken in many instances where data is to be published in the future, that revealing the data does not jeopardise the publication. Additionally your company may not wish to provide commercially sensitive data to competitors;
- ▶ If your company does not own the data, you must have the owners' permission to use it;
- ▶ Data on file can usually be supplied as a summary document but it must be a stand-alone document and contain enough information so that the reader can adequately assess the validity of any claims or statements made. It is advisable to prepare the data on file with the promotional item so that this can be reviewed and approved for release at the same time as the promotional material is being approved. As the data on file must be supplied without delay, prior preparation avoids the panic of having to prepare data on file when requested to provide it.

Superlatives and exaggerated claims `Clause 7.10`

Superlatives are grammatical expressions which denote the highest quality or degree, such as best, strongest, widest, etc. for a product. They are only allowed in the UK if they are factual statements that can be substantiated, e.g. 'the most widely prescribed'. In contrast 'the best' would not be acceptable. Examples of superlatives are claims such as:
- ▶ The best;
- ▶ The most effective;
- ▶ The most prescribed.

Even the use of the word 'the' can imply a special merit, quality or property for a medicine in certain circumstances, e.g. a claim that a product is "The anti-hypertensive" implies that it is best. This is unlikely to be an acceptable claim.

Exaggerated and all-embracing claims are not permitted. An unqualified claim that a product is 'safe' will always be considered a breach but a claim for 'unique' might, in exceptional circumstances, be defensible, e.g. 'unique mode of action or unique method of delivery' if this can be substantiated. However the argument that every product is unique in some way would not be sufficient! The particular circumstances and the evidence supporting the claim will determine whether it is judged unacceptable but here are some examples of potentially exaggerated and all embracing claims:

- ▶ Safe;
- ▶ Unique;
- ▶ The standard for;
- ▶ The number one;
- ▶ The drug of choice; and
- ▶ The gold standard.

Training `Clause 16.1`

It is a requirement of the Code that all relevant personnel are fully conversant with the Code, relevant pharmacovigilance (PV) requirements and other relevant laws and regulations. Examples of relevant staff include those in sales, marketing, medical. It also includes third party agencies engaged by the company, other contractors and consultants.

Although it is only a requirement that PV training is documented it is also advisable to keep records of ABPI Code training.

Transfers of value (ToV) `Clause 24`

ToV to healthcare professionals (HCPs) and healthcare organisations (HCOs)

The ABPI Code "applies to the promotion of medicines to members of the United Kingdom health professionals and other relevant decision makers". However there are cross border requirements which apply to disclosures of transfers of value made directly or indirectly to health professionals and healthcare organisations located in "Europe". The Code defines "Europe" as those countries that are within the European Union (EU) plus those with a national self-regulatory association that is a member of EFPIA. Disclosure is required even if the payments, etc. are made by overseas affiliates, head offices in the UK or overseas and UK based offices. Disclosure is made based on the national code where the HCP/HCO receiving transfer has their principal practice.

For example:
Italian-based European Headquarters engages and pays a consultancy fee to a HCP whose principal practice is in the UK to participate in an advisory board taking place in Germany. The Transfer of value should be disclosed under the name of recipient HCP (provided they give their consent) in the UK, following the ABPI Code.

A 'transfer of value' can be either cash or other benefit in kind provided directly or indirectly from a pharmaceutical company to a practising HCP or HCO. The term "health professional" in relation to disclosure of transfers of value also includes any employee of a pharmaceutical company whose primary occupation is that of a practising health professional (refer to **Definitions**, page 140).

A direct transfer of value is one made directly by a company for the benefit of a recipient. An indirect transfer of value is one made by a third party on behalf of a company for the benefit of a recipient where the company knows or can identify the recipient that will benefit from the transfer of value. Different categories of transfers of value to individual health professionals can be aggregated on a category by category basis, provided that itemised disclosure would be made available upon request to the relevant recipient or the relevant authorities. Payments to healthcare organisations are required to be disclosed on a per activity basis.

The following are considered transfers of value:

▶ Those made in connection with Joint working; **Clause 20**
▶ Donations, grants and benefits in kind provided to institutions, organisations and associations; **Clause 19.1, 19.2**
▶ Fees for services paid via contracts between companies and institutions, organisations and associations; **Clause 21**
▶ Financial sponsorship of attendance by health professionals and other relevant decision makers at meetings; **Clause 22.5**
▶ Consultancy fees and expenses paid to health professionals and other relevant decision makers, or to their employers on their behalf; **Clause 23.2, 23.3, 23.4**
▶ Contributions towards the costs of meetings paid to healthcare organisations or to third parties managing events on their behalf, which may include sponsorship of health professionals by way of registration fees and of registration fees and accommodation and travel.

The following are NOT transfers of value for the purposes of the Code, provided all other requirements of the Code which apply to their supply are met:

▶ Transfers of value that are solely related to over-the-counter medicines;
▶ Ordinary course purchases and sales of medicines by and between a company and a HCP or HCO including certain package deals. ToV made in the course of other package deals would need to be disclosed. However when a company employs a health professional or a healthcare organisation to provide a service as part of the package deal e.g. a nurse to administer a vaccine, then payments to the HCP or HCO must be disclosed as a ToV; **Suppl 18.1**
▶ Samples of medicines; **Clause 17**
▶ Inexpensive items which are to be passed on to patients and which are part of a formal patient support programme; **Clause 18.2**
▶ Inexpensive notebooks, pens and pencils for use at meetings. They must not bear names of products or any information about them but may bear the name of the company; **Clause 18.3**
▶ Subsistence provided to health professionals. **Clause 22.1**

Further details are available in Table 1: Summary of requirements when disclosing transfers of value to HCPs and HCOs.

ToV to Patient Organisations (POs) `Clauses 27.7, 27.8`

Transfers of value such as donations and payments for services to POs must also be disclosed. There is further information about the requirements for this disclosure in **Chapter 5: Information to General Public and Patients** and in **Table 2: Summary of requirements when disclosing transfers of value to patient organisations.**

N.B. Clause 24 of the Code does NOT apply to disclosures of transfers of value to POs.

Table 1: Summary of requirements when disclosing transfers of value to HCPs and HCOs

DATA TO BE COLLECTED	LEVEL OF DISCLOSURE	TIMING OF DISCLOSURE	ADDITIONAL INFORMATION
Donations and Grants Paid to Healthcare Organisations (HCOs) Sponsorship of or contribution to costs of events and meetings to HCOs/ third parties appointed by HCOs to manage an event • Registration fees • Travel & accommodation	Individual HCO and for each activity (Clause 24.7)	• Disclose annually in respect of each calendar year. Disclosure must be in the first six months after the end of the calendar year in which the transfers were made, i.e. in 2019 for transfers of value made in 2018 • Information must remain in the public domain for at least 3 years • Companies must document all disclosures and retain records for at least 5 years after the end of the calendar year to which they relate	• Companies must ensure that they have appropriate arrangements in place to lawfully disclose information about transfers of value and that recipients are aware of this process • There is a central platform for disclosure in the UK which companies must use. The template to be used is available from the Authority's website www. pmcpa.org.uk
Fee-for-Service and Consultancy Paid to HCO • Fees • Related expenses agreed in the fees for service or consultancy contract	Individual HCO and for each activity (Clause 24.7)		
Sponsorship of Healthcare Professional (HCP) To Attend Meetings and Events • Registration fees • Travel & accommodation (inside & outside UK)	Individual HCP		
Fees Paid to HCPs (or other relevant decision makers) for Service and Consultancy • Fees • Related expenses agreed in the fees for service or consultancy contract This includes payments made to UK consultants taking part in market research, even for the one-off market research. Except when the company is not aware of the identities of those participating in the market research.	Individual HCP		
Transfers of Value in Accordance With Joint Working • The financial amount or value and the name of the recipient. Companies must ensure that the amount spent on joint working projects is made public irrespective of whether the value is transferred to a healthcare organisation or some other funding model is used.	Individual Joint Working (JW) Project		
Research & Development **Transfer of value to HCPs/HCOs related to the planning and conduct of:** • Non-clinical studies (as defined in the OECD Principles of GLP) • Clinical trials (as defined in Directive 2001/20/EC) • Non-interventional studies that are prospective in nature and that involve the collection of patient data from or on behalf of individual, or groups of, HCPs specifically for the study Costs that are subsidiary to these activities can be included in the aggregate amount.	Aggregate		

Table 2: Summary of requirements when disclosing transfers of value to patient organisations

DATA TO BE COLLECTED	LEVEL OF DISCLOSURE	TIMING OF DISCLOSURE
Donations to POs List the patient organisations at a national or European level which it has provided: • Financial support and/or • Significant indirect/non-financial support The published information must include the monetary value of financial support and of invoiced costs.	Individual PO	• The list of organisations being provided with support during a calendar year must be disclosed annually within six months of the year end in which the ToVs were made. The description of the support must be sufficiently complete to enable the average reader to form an understanding of the significance of the support • For significant non-financial support that cannot be assigned a meaningful monetary value, the published information must describe clearly the non-monetary value that the organisation receives
Fees Paid to POs for Services List the patient organisations at a national or European level which it has engaged to provide: • Significant contracted services, which must include a description of the nature of the services provided that is sufficiently complete to enable the average reader to form an understanding of the arrangement without the necessity to divulge confidential information • Companies must also make publicly available the total amount paid per patient organisation over the reporting period	Individual PO	• The list of organisations engaged must be updated at least once a year • This must include a description of the nature of the services provided that is sufficiently complete to enable the average reader to form an understanding of the arrangement without the necessity to divulge confidential information • Companies must also make publicly available the total amount paid per patient organisation over the reporting period

CHAPTER **2**

Meetings and Congresses

Main clauses: 10, 12, 22, 23

Both promotional and non-promotional meetings are covered under the scope of the ABPI Code of Practice:

▶ Promotional (e.g. sales-representative organised meetings);
▶ Non-promotional (e.g. non-product educational meetings, advisory boards and investigator meetings for clinical studies).

The 2019 Code has clarified when the arrangements for meetings involving travel outside the UK require certification or examination. Refer to **Chapter 1: Basic Principles – Certification and examination** for details.

Corporate hospitality which is not associated with an allowable event should not be provided to healthcare professionals, patient groups etc., although it can be given and received as part of normal business activities that fall outside the scope of the Code, e.g. relationships with vendors, such as those providing computer services.

Congresses are meetings that are organised independently rather than by pharmaceutical companies, although companies will often sponsor them. International congresses are usually held in a different country each year and are intended for an international audience. National meetings of organisations are usually intended mainly for an audience from a particular country. The difference between international congresses and national congresses is important and will be discussed further in the relevant sections.

Promotional meetings `Clauses 10, 12, 18, 22, 23`

Company-organised promotional meetings are allowed but the ABPI requires that the company's involvement in the meeting is transparent. The primary purpose of the meeting must be its educational content. It is useful to state the educational aims in the invitation and these must be met. Note that a meeting may be highly scientific and may provide good quality educational content but it can still be promotional. The judgements on promotional versus non-promotional, and scientific and educational versus non-scientific are separate albeit related.

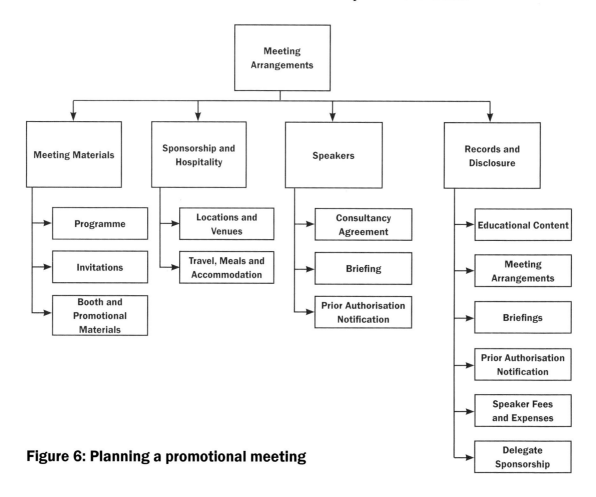

Figure 6: Planning a promotional meeting

Learning from a Case: Auth/2331/7/10 – Educational presentation in promotional meeting
An invitation was sent by a pharmaceutical company with a covering letter which clearly described a meeting as promotional and sponsored by a pharmaceutical company. An educational presentation given at the meeting focused on an off-label indication of the product concerned. The Panel ruled that both recipients of the invitation and delegates would inevitably associate the product with this off-label indication and that this presentation made the promotion of the product inconsistent with its licence.
Learning Point:
• Don't try to integrate promotional and non-promotional meetings.

Examples of promotional meetings include:

- ▶ Sales representative-organised lunchtime and evening meetings, e.g. local meeting for GPs or hospital departments;
- ▶ Large national product launch meetings;
- ▶ 'Roadshows' product launch or new-indication promotional meetings held at various venues around the country.

Hints & Tips
For any hospitality think IMPRESSION, IMPRESSION, IMPRESSION. If this meeting is made public, for example if it appears in the press or a competitor finds out, will your company (and the MHRA and PMCPA) be happy with the impression it creates????

There may or may not be a company stand or booth at the meeting. This may range from a small table-top stand to a large walk-on structure with advertising panels. All promotional material must meet the requirements of the ABPI Code.

Impression

The first and last thing to think about when organising a meeting is the IMPRESSION that is going to be created. Ask yourself the following questions:

- ▶ If the details of this meeting were to be described fairly in the tabloid press what impression would it give?
- ▶ Would you, your company, the regulators and self-regulatory bodies be happy with the impression created?

If the answers are that the details of the meeting would give a bad impression then the arrangements are not compliant and should be changed.

Meeting materials

Numerous types of materials are associated with a promotional meeting, for example:

- ▶ Programme;
- ▶ Invitations and welcome letters;
- ▶ Booth panels and other promotional materials;
- ▶ Powerpoint presentations and videos;
- ▶ Presentation notes and handouts for delegates;
- ▶ Post-meeting report.

All materials must be consistent with the licence and meet the requirements of the ABPI Code, they must be reviewed and individually certified as standalone items. Refer to **Chapter 3: Printed Materials – Tables 7, 8 and 9** for details of requirements Additionally all materials must make it clear that it is a company-organised meeting.

N.B. The company is also responsible for any materials produced by third parties, e.g. welcome letters from the conference organiser. These must all comply with the Code and be approved by the pharmaceutical company.

Hints & Tips
Document the educational purpose when starting to plan the meeting and make this clear in the invitations.

Programme

The programme must be planned so that it is consistent with the terms of the marketing authorisation(s) of the product. It must be approved and certified in the same way as other printed promotional materials.

Hints & Tips
State clearly in the meeting invitation that it is only open to invited HCPs. This can avoid embarrassment when ineligible persons attempt to gain entry.

Educational content

Education must be the primary purpose of a meeting. It is useful to state the educational aims in the invitation and these must be met.

Invitations

Only healthcare professionals and other relevant decision makers can be invited. Delegates, with the exception of speakers, cannot be paid to attend a meeting. It is not permissible to pay journalists or to make payments for locum cover during a healthcare professional's absence.

Booth and promotional materials

If the venue is in a public place, e.g. an hotel, care must be taken to ensure that the booth and any materials are not accessible by the general public.

Refer to Table 4: Planning promotional materials for booths at international congresses and Table 6 : Planning promotional materials for booths at national congresses and meetings.

Sponsorship and hospitality

Location and venues

The location must be as convenient as possible for the majority of the attendees. When choosing a location ensure that local meetings are held locally and regional or national meetings are held in as convenient a place as possible, for the majority of attendees in terms of travel links. There must be a 'valid and cogent' reason for a meeting being allowed to take place outside of the home country, i.e. outside of UK, if the part of the company organising the meeting is based in the UK. Examples of valid reasons might be:

- ▶ The meeting is being held before, during or after an international congress;
- ▶ The meeting is being held where the resource or expertise that is the object or subject matter of the meeting is located. For example, the company's research facility;
- ▶ The location makes the most sense logistically, e.g. most of the attendees are located outside of the country of the company organising the meeting.

It would not be permissible just because one of the speakers is located in that place or country.

The venue must be:

- ▶ Appropriate, for example there must be a private room where the meeting can

Key Point
It is still classed as a meeting if even only one or two pharmaceutical company personnel meet with a healthcare professional. However a sales representative's day-to-day call would not usually be classed as a meeting for these purposes.

be held which is not open to the general public;

Hints & Tips
When choosing a location ensure that local meetings are held in as convenient a place as possible for the majority of attendees.

▶ Conducive to the main purpose of the meeting. Education is the main purpose of the event and so the facility must be sufficiently quiet to be suitable to facilitate this purpose.

Finally, think about the IMPRESSION that the venue would create if the details of the meeting were to become known to the general public. It must NOT be renowned for its entertainment facilities, for example:

▶ A hotel associated with a golf course;
▶ A theme park;
▶ A spa hotel;
▶ A football, rugby or cricket stadium;
▶ A greyhound or horse racing stadium;
▶ Motor or bike racing track.

Nor extravagant, lavish or deluxe, for example:

▶ Famous restaurants where it is difficult to get a reservation;
▶ Hotels famous for their opulence.

Although that said, there has been at least one case brought under the UK ABPI Code of Practice where a meeting that used a sporting facility was not found to have breached the Code. This was because it had been selected because it had good conference facilities and there wasn't a sporting event taking place at the time of the meeting. Another reason for selecting such a venue (in addition to the excellent conference facilities) may be that it may be that it is the only venue in the vicinity large enough to accommodate the meeting. However no sporting activities must be taking place on the day of the meeting.

Sometimes sales representatives hold small lunchtime meetings in doctors' surgeries or postgraduate medical centres. Whilst payment for room rental in the postgraduate centres in hospitals is permitted, payment must not be made in the UK under any circumstances to general practitioners for room rental.

Travel, meals and accommodation

The guidance with respect to food and drink provided by pharmaceutical companies for

Learning from a Case: Auth/2621/7/13 – Late night drinks are not subsistence
Company employees bought drinks in a hotel bar late at night for meeting delegates, while awaiting the arrival of a taxi. Late night drinks were ruled not to come within the definition of subsistence as allowed under the code and a breach was ruled.
Learning Point:
• You must only provide food and drink which can be truly considered as 'subsistence'.

healthcare professionals is that it should not be lavish but should be of a standard that the health professional would pay for themselves. The ABPI Code refers to food and drink as subsistence.The cost of a meal (including drinks) provided as subsistence must not exceed £75 per person, excluding VAT

Hints & Tips
Ensure all arrangements are well-documented from the outset and this documentation is retained.

and gratuities. Normally costs will be well below this figure, this maximum is only appropriate in very exceptional circumstances, e.g. at a residential meeting for senior consultants or dinner at a learned society conference.

Refreshments should not be provided to spouses who are not *bona fide* delegates at the meeting. Alcohol should only be provided in limited amounts during the meal and it is not permissible for drinks to be bought in the bar afterwards.

Overnight accommodation can only be provided to *bona fide* delegates (not spouses or partners) and only if the educational content of the meeting cannot be provided without it. The criterion is the length of the working day, which is a combination of the travel time and the amount of educational content. If travel and the educational content can be achieved without an overnight stay, then the accommodation cannot be justified. If accommodation has been provided then a rule of thumb is that a minimum of approximately 6 hours educational content must be provided on the second day.

Assuming Code requirements for the choice of location of the promotional meeting have been followed (Refer to **Location and venues** page 34) travel expenses may be met for *bona fide* delegates (not spouses or partners, unless they are delegates in their own right). The following apply:

- ▶ Air travel for delegates must be limited to economy class unless the flight is scheduled to take longer than 6 hours in which case premium economy or similar may be provided;
- ▶ The ABPI Code does not specifically prohibit first class rail travel and cost and travel time would need to be taken into account in deciding acceptability;
- ▶ Travel for consultants engaged by the company, e.g. speakers may be business class if the company's own standard operating procedures (SOPs) permit.

Speakers

External speakers – consultancy agreement

When external consultants are engaged as speakers a written consultancy agreement must be drawn up and a record of the agreement must be kept. For more details refer to **Chapter 1: Basic Principles – Consultancy agreement**.

N.B. If a company employs a practising HCP on a part-time basis, they must ensure that the HCP is obliged to declare this employment whenever they write or speak on a subject which is connected to that employment or the company employing them.

Speaker briefings and slide approval

The following should be considered when arranging speakers for company meetings:

- ▶ Both internal company speakers and external speakers must be briefed and records of this briefing must be kept;
- ▶ A consultancy agreement must be set up for external speakers;
- ▶ Payments to external speakers must not exceed fair market value (FMV). Delegates cannot be paid to attend the meeting;
- ▶ All presentations must be certified that they are consistent with the marketing authorisation and meet the requirements of the applicable codes.

Prior authorisation/notification

The prior authorisation or notification of authorities or employers for healthcare professionals to attend meetings is not a requirement of the ABPI Code in the UK. It is a requirement in some European countries and this may have to be factored into plans when UK companies are organising pan-European company meetings.

Records and disclosures

Records

Adequate records must be kept of all arrangements connected to the meeting and these may need to be produced in the event of a complaint about the meeting. These records must include the following:

- ▶ Educational content (e.g. copy of the programme and the presentations);
- ▶ Meeting arrangements
  - – Venue and location
  - – Costs
  - – List of invitees and attendees;
- ▶ Consultancy agreements and speaker briefings;
- ▶ Prior authorisation/notification of authorities (if applicable);
- ▶ Speaker fees and expenses;
- ▶ Delegate sponsorship.

Disclosures

Companies must document and publicly disclose certain transfers of value, e.g. consultancy fees and sponsorship paid directly or indirectly to health professionals and healthcare organisations located in Europe. Refer to Table 1: Summary of requirements when disclosing transfers of value to HCPs and HCOs for further information.

Company-organised non-promotional meetings

Companies can organise non-product related educational/scientific/medical meetings that are non-promotional. These can be local, national or international. Examples include updates on a therapeutic area and training on aspects of running a general practice. Just because a company has organised a meeting does not mean that it is classified as promotional. Nevertheless, if the company's product features at all in the content then it may well become a promotional meeting. A passing mention by an independent speaker of the company's product alongside several others may not be sufficient to 'cross the line' but great care is necessary in organising all company meetings. It is particularly important to avoid the promotion of unlicensed products or indications at company meetings. All the requirements concerning hospitality, venue, etc. which apply to promotional meetings also apply to non-promotional meetings.

Advisory board meetings Clause 22, 23, 24

Pharmaceutical companies set up advisory boards for the purpose, as the name suggests, of getting advice on a particular aspect of the development or commercialisation of their products. Advisors or consultants generally advise the pharmaceutical company on marketing and clinical issues and help to answer questions so the company can better direct medical, clinical and marketing efforts. Advisory boards are, therefore, for the benefit of the company and the participants are usually paid for their services which must be delivered under the terms of a contract.

Advisory boards are not considered as promotional and differ from other types of company organised meetings that do have an educational content and are considered promotional. However, advisory boards must be organised appropriately and their objectives clearly defined or they may be considered promotion or disguised promotion. The organisation of the advisory board and the rationale for it must be able to stand up to independent scrutiny.

Any company personnel attending the advisory board should attend in a non-promotional role and for this reason, members of the sales force should not normally attend advisory boards.

Records and disclosure

Consultancy agreements and payments

It is usual for members of advisory boards to be paid a consultancy fee and this must now be laid down in a formal contract. The fee should be in line with professional rates of remuneration and should reflect the amount of time spent in the advisory capacity.

Public Disclosure of Fees

Companies must document and publicly disclose certain transfers of value, e.g. consultancy fees paid directly or indirectly to health professionals and healthcare organisations located in Europe. Refer to Table 1: Summary of requirements when disclosing transfers of value to HCPs and HCOs for further information.

Selection and invitation of members

Number and who to invite

Advisors must be selected based upon their knowledge, experience or other skill-based qualification that will allow the objectives of the advisory board to be met. They must not be selected on the basis of their history of, or potential for, prescribing the pharmaceutical company's products. This is to ensure that the event is not designed to promote the use of the

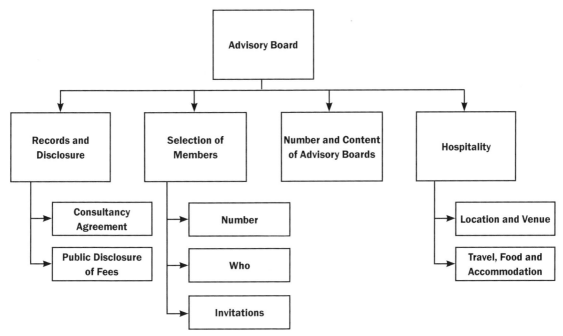

Figure 7: Organising an advisory board

company's products. However, there could be some topics on which the company needs advice that require the advisors to have certain experience (and, therefore, prescribing potential), e.g. experience of a particular disease.

The number of advisors/consultants selected for any one advisory board meeting should not be too numerous both for the sake of efficiency and from an ethical perspective. A large number of invitees may give the impression that the company is pursuing commercial objectives and the meeting is disguised promotion. The number invited should, therefore, be limited to a number that could reasonably contribute in an interactive forum and should not be greater than the number really needed to obtain the advice sought. This number is not specified in most countries. If the disease area involves different specialties or professions then representation from the various groups should be considered.

Learning from a Case: Auth/2747/1/15 – Selection of members for advisory board
This case concerned a large meeting, involving over 100 HCPs from several different countries, where Phase II data on an unapproved indication was presented. The panel noted that the meeting design did not allow delegates to provide advice and consequently this was not a genuine advisory board and was disguised promotion of an unlicensed indication. A breach of clause 2 and a requirement for a corrective statement were also ruled.
Learning Points:
*   It is acceptable to hold multiple country advisory boards in one location. However, the sole purpose of an advisory board should be to gain advice from the participants. The presentation of current data should not be an objective of the meeting. Otherwise it is highly likely a breach of clause 2 will be ruled.
*   The time spent obtaining advice should be higher than 50% of the total meeting time. Q & A sessions should aim to obtain advice not to train the delegates on data.
*   Delegate selection should always be made on the basis of expertise never on the potential to prescribe.

Invitations

Invitations must make it clear that it is an invitation to participate in an advisory board. The objectives of the meeting and what the advisor is expected to do at the meeting (and possibly in preparation) should be made clear. It is good practice to include an agenda.

Although the advisory board is not promotional (if it is organised correctly), the initial invitation is potentially subject to the rules on promotional items. It is considered to be the same as any mailing to a healthcare professional as the invitee may ultimately not want to participate in the advisory board. This can present a dilemma because the objectives of the advisory board must be made clear in the invitation but advisory boards can discuss off-label or unlicensed uses of products. However it is important that the invitation does not promote a product in an unlicensed or off-label manner. The reason for this is that the invitation is sent in advance of the consultancy agreement being established and an invitation which is, in effect, itself promotional would be seen as unlicensed or off-label promotion.

Number and content of advisory boards

The number of advisory boards held should not be so many as to be construed as disguised promotion. Taken together with the number of attendees at each event, the total number of advisors consulted should not be greater than is really needed to provide the advice that the company seeks.

If the advisory board is correctly organised, the content is not normally considered promotional. It can be legitimate for unlicensed and off-label information to be discussed at the advisory board. However, care must be taken in the organisation of the meeting that the content is not allowed to slip into the promotional arena.

It may well be necessary to provide the advisors with information and data on unlicensed or licensed products prior to obtaining their advice but the balance of the meeting must be very clearly information-receiving not information-giving. It is not acceptable to add on a feedback session at the end of an information-giving meeting in an attempt to re-classify it as an advisory board.

Therefore it is important to avoid the following:
- ▶ Frequent use and prominently displayed brand names on communication material such as presentation slides;
- ▶ An accent on presentations, with prominence devoted to the presentation of data rather than an interactive discussion.

Learning from a Case: Auth/2493/3/12 – Selection of members for advisory board
The arrangements for advisory boards were challenged. Most were found to be acceptable but the company was found in breach because a practice manager advisory board invitation was distributed too widely without specific named addressees.
Learning Point:
- You should select specific invitees to match closely your stated learning objectives.

Branded pens and pads are no longer allowed to be provided, but pens and pads for use at the meeting bearing the company name are allowed up to a perceived value of £6.

Hospitality during advisory board meetings

This is, in general, the same as for hospitality at other types of meetings the exception to this is that advisory board members are not restricted to economy-class air travel, as would be the case for delegates to other meetings (unless the flight is scheduled to take longer than 6 hours in which case premium economy or similar may be provided.). More information can be found in the section **Promotional Meetings: Sponsorship and hospitality** page 34.

International congresses

International congresses are meetings that are organised independently rather than by pharmaceutical companies, although companies will often sponsor these. They are usually held in a different country each year and are intended for an international audience; examples would be European Thoracic Society meeting (ETS), American Academy of Dermatology (AAD) or the World Congress of AIDS (WAIDS). Note that although some congresses are called 'American ...' or 'European ...' the delegate base may in reality be truly international. The attendee profile is sometimes more important than the title. However, national meetings of organisations are usually intended mainly for an audience from a particular country; for example the British Thoracic Society (BTS) or the British HIV Association (BHIVA) are primarily intended for a British audience, and the German AIDS Society (DAH) is primarily intended for a German audience.

This difference, between international congresses and national congresses, is important because the ABPI Code allows medicines that are either not licensed or not licensed for a particular indication in the UK to be promoted at international congresses held in the UK, provided all of the following requirements of the Code are met:

- ▶ The product is licensed in another major industrialised country;
- ▶ The meeting is a *bona fide* international meeting and is of a high scientific standing;
- ▶ A significant proportion of the delegates are from counties where the product is licensed;
- ▶ All materials clearly state:
  - The product is not licensed in the UK
  - The names of the countries in which the product is licensed
  - That registration conditions differ from country to country;
- ▶ The product or indication is relevant and proportional to the meeting.

However, although this approach is endorsed by the EFPIA[2,6,7] and IFPMA codes[8] this is not reflected in some other European countries and this must be taken into account if a UK company is planning activities at international congresses in other European countries, e.g. Germany where where the legal interpretation of the law which prohibits promotion of an unlicensed product is particularly strict.

Organisation for pharmaceutical companies attending international congresses is often handled centrally, either via a European, international or global headquarters and broadly falls into the categories in **Figure 8: Planning international congresses**. Before considering these categories there are several important points that must be taken into account:

- ▶ The congress organiser's rules;
- ▶ The location of the congress (is it inside or outside Europe and which country);
- ▶ The applicable national code.

Location of the congress

The EFPIA Code requires that promotion, which takes place within Europe, must comply with:

- ▶ Applicable laws and regulations;
- ▶ National code of the country in which the promotion takes place;

PLUS for a European company

- ▶ National code where company is located;

OR for a non-European company

- ▶ The EFPIA Code.

Although not specified in the EFPIA code, the national code, regulations and requirements of the home country of each invited participant should also be considered.

This means that different rules apply depending on where the company is located. European-located companies must apply their home country code in addition to the host country code. In practice this means that, for example, at a congress held elsewhere in Europe, UK-located companies cannot run competitions on an exhibition stand. The codes of some other countries do not specify this rule hence companies based elsewhere in Europe may be able to run such competitions.

The determination of where a company is located is not straightforward and the EFPIA Code refers to the 'legal entity' that organises or sponsors promotion or engages in HCP interactions. This suggests that a European HQ responsible for activities at an international congress must apply the ABPI Code if they are based in the UK.

Note however that the EFPIA Code confirms that the arrangements for funding attendance of HCPs at international meetings must comply with the code in the country that the HCP carries out their profession. You should not arrange conference attendance for HCPs based outside the UK without checking arrangements with your responsible affiliate company (see **Sponsorship and Hospitality** section).

The EFPIA on-line platform (www.efpia-e4ethics.eu) is a tool to pre-assess events in regard of EFPIA's HCP Code. Reports will be shared with corporate compliance officers, the National Ethics Groups, and congress and meeting organisers to promote compliance with industry standards. EFPIA has also begun the monitoring of congress activities, including exhibitions at congresses, drawing company compliance officers' attention to problematic behaviour.

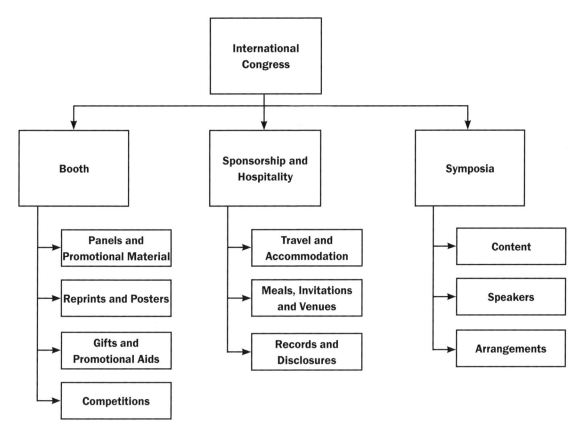

Figure 8: Planning international congresses

Booths

Promotional materials including booth panels

The promotional materials that are used by pharmaceutical company staff at their company booth to advertise products to the conference delegates at international congresses must be produced, and certified for use, in accordance with the legal and self-regulatory frameworks in the applicable countries. These promotional materials include: printed detail aids, electronic detail aids, leave pieces and product monographs. The checklist **Table 4: Planning promotional materials for booths at international congresses** is intended as a prompt for what needs to be considered when producing both promotional materials and booth panels, and the column on the right is a quick reference guide to where this information can be found.

Reprints and posters

The distribution of reprints of clinical papers or posters by sales representatives in a booth is regarded as promotional. Therefore only reprints and posters that are within the terms of the licence may be used. In many countries they must be certified as promotional items. The ABPI Code states that only peer-reviewed articles can be provided proactively. If there is a separate medical information portion of the booth, then reprints and posters can usually be provided whether or not they fall within the scope of the licence if they are used to answer unsolicited questions. See **Table 3: Reprints and posters distributed at international congress booths** for some practical checks.

Gifts and promotional aids

Gifts are not allowed anywhere in Europe. The ABPI Code does not even allow items bearing a company name for patient use (which are still allowed in some other circumstances) to be given out from a booth, although they may be exhibited for later delivery. This prohibition includes providing gifts indirectly through sponsorship, for example conference bags and pass-holders, even if these are distributed via the conference organisers themselves. It also covers services which provide a benefit to recipients (e.g. internet access on a booth) as well as physical items, e.g. notebooks, pens and pencils which should NEVER be provided from exhibition booths.

N.B. Although pads and pens or pencils MUST NOT be provided from a booth, they may be provided (by one or more companies) in just a few exceptional circumstances, e.g. in conference bags or during a meeting or symposia. According to the ABPI Code total cost of the items provided to an individual recipient must not exceed a perceived value of £6, excluding VAT (other European Codes have different thresholds for this value). An individual attendee should not receive more than one notebook and one pen or pencil. However, Code requirements vary depending on how they are supplied:

Pads, pens or pencils supplied at a company organised scientific meeting, congress or promotional meeting:

> ► MUST NOT bear a product name or any information about a product but MAY bear a Company name.

Pads, pens or pencils provided in conference bags at third party-organised meetings:

> ► MUST NOT include the name of the donor company or companies, product name or any information about a product.

Competitions

The use of competitions and quizzes is generally considered an unacceptable method of promotion under the ABPI Code. Quizzes are allowed in some restricted circumstances such as during the formal proceedings of a meeting but never from a promotional booth. Refer to **Chapter 6: Goods, Services & Donations – Competitions** for more information.

Learning from a Case: Auth/2234/5/09 - Unlicensed promotion
A breach of Clause 2 was ruled because a symposium on diabetes care sponsored by a pharmaceutical company which concluded with a keynote lecture 'A New Molecule in Diabetes - From Conception to Reality' delivered by a company employee. This constituted promotion of an unlicensed product.
Although information about a product can be provided under certain circumstances, e.g. legitimate scientific exchange at some congresses.
Learning Points:
- A product must never be promoted prior to its marketing authorization and care must be taken that promotion is not disguised as 'scientific exchange'.
- Using a company employee as a speaker may mean the presentation is viewed as promotion.

Sponsorship and hospitality

Pharmaceutical companies sometimes sponsor delegates to attend international congresses. This may be simply paying for one or all of the following:

- ▶ Travel and accommodation;
- ▶ Meals or a meal;
- ▶ Conference registration fees.

This type of sponsorship is allowed under the ABPI Code provided that the restrictions described below on class of air travel, accommodation and venues for dinner are met.

Neither the ABPI Code nor the MHRA requires prior notification or requires permission to be sought from employers for healthcare professionals when sponsored to attend a congress. This is not true for some other European countries, therefore if a UK company is organising congress attendance for other European HCPs, one of the first considerations is whether the authorities in the health professional's country require notification of this sponsorship. For example, this is true in France where the National Medical Board, Conseil National de l'Ordre des Médecins (CNOM), and the National Board of Pharmacists, Conseil National de l'Ordre des Pharmaciens (CNOP), require 30 days' advance notification of hospitality or sponsorship. Some countries, e.g. Sweden and The Netherlands, require part payment by the HCP so similar considerations apply. Always check arrangements with your affiliated company in the HCP's home country.

Travel and accommodation

Pharmaceutical companies may pay or reimburse UK delegates attending international congresses for reasonable travel expenses but any air travel can only be economy class unless the flight is scheduled to take longer than 6 hours in which case premium economy or similar may be provided. This restriction does not apply to those who are attending the meeting to provide consultancy services to the company, for example, speakers at the company sponsored symposia may be allowed to travel business class provided the pharmaceutical companies own policies permit this class of travel.

The ABPI Code does not specifically prohibit first class rail travel and cost and travel time would need to be taken into account in deciding acceptability.

Learning from a Case: Auth/2546/11/12 – Sponsorship declaration
10 companies were ruled in breach of the Code because they sponsored an independent medical society meeting that included elements that breached the Code, e.g. golf and an extravagant gala dinner. The companies hadn't actually sponsored the unacceptable activities but this wasn't clear from the programme.
Learning Points:
- You must ensure that materials associated with meetings you sponsor make clear the nature of your support.
- General acknowledgements of sponsorship may mean you are blamed for unacceptable elements in independent meetings.

If any of the delegates are local to the congress venue then accommodation would not be deemed necessary and it would not be compliant with the Code to provide it in such circumstances. However it is likely that for many delegates to international congresses overnight accommodation will be necessary due to the logistics of the travel time to the congress. The hotel chosen should not be extravagant, lavish or deluxe and for this reason many companies policies state that hotels they pay for must be four stars or below.

Costs for travel, accommodation or meals for accompanying persons, such as spouses, who do not qualify as delegates in their own right cannot be paid by a pharmaceutical company. It is a good idea to state this on any invitations.

Meals

Meals must not be lavish and be of a 'reasonable' level and not exceed the standard that the HCP would pay for themselves. The EFPIA Code states that the national association Codes must set a monetary threshold with respect to food and drink provided by pharmaceutical companies for HCPs. The ABPI Code has set this threshold at a maximum of £75 per person, excluding VAT and gratuities. The ABPI Code states that normally costs should be well below this figure, this maximum is only appropriate in very exceptional circumstances, e.g. at a residential meeting for senior consultants or dinner at a learned society conference.

The national association or 'country' codes have set their thresholds in very different places and this was resulting in difficulties for pharmaceutical companies when providing meals at meetings which involved HCPs from a variety of countries. Under normal circumstances when more than one country code applies, EFPIA states that whichever is strictest should be followed. However, in practice this meant that if the congress was being held in a country with a high cost of living, it was not always possible to buy a meal if attendees were present from a country with a lower cost of living. The EFPIA Code provided a pragmatic solution to this problem by allowing an exception to the rule of "the strictest applies" in this instance; allowing the applicable threshold to be that of the host country.

Records and disclosure

If meals are within this reasonable limit there is no need for them to be disclosed as a 'transfer of value'. However, companies must make the financial details of sponsorship of UK health professionals and other relevant decision makers publicly available. Refer to **Table 1: Summary of requirements when disclosing transfers of value to HCPs and HCOs** for further information.

Symposia

Pharmaceutical companies may organise a satellite symposium at a third-party-organised scientific congress or convention. Such meetings are not independent in the same way as third party congress or conventions organised by a medical or scientific association or society. These symposia are subject to close scrutiny from the regulatory authorities, self-regulatory authorities and competitors. The pharmaceutical company will be considered responsible for the actions of its employees and any third parties acting on their behalf, e.g. Key Opinion Leader (KOL) speakers and agencies.

New clinical data relating to unapproved uses or indications may be presented at these meetings as part of a legitimate scientific exchange. However, it is not permitted for this to be promotional in any way. The licence status of the product MUST be clearly stated by the presenters within the presentations.

Breaches of the Code have been ruled when promotion has been disguised as 'scientific exchange'. Therefore, in order to avoid breaching the law and Codes of conduct, the following guidance should be followed:

Content of symposium

Branding and logos

The presentations delivered and any other materials used at the symposium must not contain trade names, branding or logos.

Accurate

The information presented during the symposium must be checked for medical and scientific accuracy, i.e. all statements, figures, statistical information and references. There must not be any commercial input into the content of the speakers' presentations.

Balanced

It is particularly important that the information presented must be fair and balanced in all ways. The following should be considered:

- ▶ The body of evidence in this therapeutic area, any statements made MUST be representative of this opinion;
- ▶ It is not acceptable at a pharmaceutical company symposium to present data which although accurate contradicts or does not concur with the results of the majority of similar studies;
- ▶ It must be made clear to the audience, when the data is being presented, if it is an area of emerging opinion.

There isn't any definitive guidance for the amount of time that can be taken up by presenting data on the company's product, but balance should also be provided within the symposium in terms of overall content without undue emphasis being placed on information regarding the company's pre-licence product. Otherwise it may give the appearance of promoting a product before its Marketing Authorization has been granted or outside of the terms of its Marketing Authorization.

Speakers

Records, consultancy agreements and public disclosure of fees

These will usually be independent consultants engaged by the company. If employees speak in these symposia, this may result in the presentation being viewed as promotion. (Refer to **Learning from a Case 2234/5/09.**) Consultant speakers must:

- ▶ Have a signed consultancy agreement;
- ▶ Be briefed and records of this briefing retained;
- ▶ Be paid to reflect but not exceed FMV for the service they are providing.

Companies must make the financial details of consultancy fees paid to UK health professionals and other relevant decision makers publicly available. Refer to Table 1: Summary of requirements when disclosing transfers of value to HCPs and HCOs for further information.

Arrangements

The arrangements for company satellite symposia must comply with certain conditions in order for them to be seen as suitable vehicles for the 'exchange of legitimate scientific information' and not be classed as promotional meetings. Company satellite symposia should be arranged as part of the official congress programme as opposed to being arranged by the company before, during or after the conference. Breaches of the Code have been ruled where companies have disguised company meetings as being connected to scientific congresses. Invitations to the meeting should be open to all *bona fide* attendees of the congress and not controlled by the company.

The requirements of accreditation bodies for Continuing Medical Education should also be considered if this is being sought for the event. These can include a requirement to separate any advertising material from the scientific content in meeting materials such as programmes.

Table 3: Reprints and posters distributed at international congress booths

KEY ISSUE	REFERENCE IN BOOK/CHECKLIST
Is the reprint or poster within the terms of the product licence in the applicable country?	Check with company national regulatory department or Summary of Product Characteristics for the country where the conference is being held.
If not, is it within the licence in any country and what are the rules about promotion of unlicensed/off-label information in the country where the congress is being held?	Check the legal and Code requirements with the local operating company/affiliate in the country where the congress is being held.
Check that the reprint/poster gives a balanced/accurate view of the available information?	
Could the reprint or poster be considered to be misleading?	Refer to Basic Principles: Exaggerated, false or misleading claims.
Has the paper been published in a peer-reviewed journal/independently refereed?	Many Codes require that only peer reviewed papers are supplied proactively.
Do the applicable codes require prescribing information to be supplied with the reprint?	The 2019 ABPI Code requires prescribing information to be provided when a reprint is provided proactively such as from commercial booths. Confirm local requirements but remember EFPIA rule of strictest applies if there is a difference.

Table 4: Planning promotional materials for booths at international congresses

ACTION/CHECKLIST	REFERENCE IN BOOK
Is the product or indication licensed in the country where the conference is being held?	*Check with the company's national regulatory department or Summary of Product Characteristics for the country where the conference is being held.*
If not, is it within the licence in any country and what are the rules about promotion of unlicensed/ off-label information in the country where the congress is being held?	*Check the legal and Code requirements with the local operating company/affiliate in the country where the congress is being held.*
Do the materials have to be pre-approved or submitted to the Ministry of Health in any of the countries where they are to be used?	*Check this with the local operating company/affiliate in the country where the congress is being held.*
Does the information have to be in the language where the product is licensed?	*Check with local operating company/affiliate in the country where the congress is being held.*
If licensed, are any claims consistent with the licence?	*Check with company national regulatory department or Summary of Product Characteristics for the country where the conference is being held.*
Are the claims accurate, balanced, based on up-to-date information, capable of substantiation?	*UK requirements: Basic Principles: Substantiation.*
Check what types of references are allowed as standard of proof for substantiation of claim, e.g. is data on file allowed? Some countries only allow peer reviewed published data to be used to substantiate claims.	*Check the requiremets with the local operating company/affiliate in the country where the congress is being held.*
If planning to use the word 'new' check when the word can be used.	*Check the requiremets with the local operating company/affiliate in the country where the congress is being held.*
Check what the relevant code(s) say regarding hanging comparatives, superlatives and quotes.	*For UK requirements, refer to the relevant sections in Basic Principles.*
Check that artwork such as graphs and statistics are not misleading.	*Refer to Basic Principles: Graphs.*
Does the Code specify that a unique identification number is required to be printed on the promotional piece?	*The ABPI Code in the UK requires that when items are certified they are given a unique number and this number should appear on promotional items (see Basic Principles: Unique reference).*
Is a warning symbol required, e.g. black triangle for adverse events?	*Check with local operating company/affiliate (see Basic Principles: Black triangle for UK requirements).*
Is information on how to report adverse events required?	*Check with local operating company/affiliate (refer to Basic Principles: Adverse Events mandatory warning) for UK requirements.*
Is there a requirement for prescribing information to be an integral part of the promotional item/booth panel? And if so, what must this contain?	*The ABPI Code requires PI to be either on the panels or available at the booth (if the latter, a statement is required on the panel to this effect). It is usually required for other materials. Refer to Chapter 3: Printed Materials and Chapter 7: Digital Media for exact requirements. Check with local operating company/affiliate for requirements where congress is being held.*

Although information about a product can be provided under certain circumstances, e.g. legitimate scientific exchange at some congresses, a product must never be promoted prior to its marketing authorization and care must be taken that promotion is not disguised as 'scientific exchange'.

Symposium abstract books

There should not be any reference in writing to the name (either brand or generic name) of an unlicensed product or mention of the use of a licensed product for an unlicensed indication. These materials must not be branded or contain logos.

Invitations to symposia

Invitations to symposia at international congresses may be ruled as promotional and if a product and claim are mentioned in this case they must meet the requirements of a promotional item and will need prescribing information. Additionally they are often distributed by being included in the conference bag which all delegates receive and because some delegates are not HCPs, this may mean that a prescription-only medicine (POM) is being promoted to the general public. It is usual, therefore, for these reasons, for companies to ensure that symposia invitations are non-promotional and just give details of the topic, venue and date of the symposium.

National congresses and meetings in the UK

Promotion at national congresses and meetings in the UK must be consistent with the terms of the licence of the product or products, otherwise the arrangements for international congresses can be followed. The following key issue checklists refer to promotional items, including the booth panels that are to be used in national congresses held in the UK. **N.B.** Companies cannot provide gifts such as conference bags and pass holders. (Refer also to the requirements of printed materials found in **Chapter 3: Printed Materials**.)

Table 5: Reprints distributed from booths at national congresses and meetings

KEY ISSUE	REFERENCE IN BOOK/CHECKLIST
Is the reprint within the terms of the product licence?	Check with company national regulatory department or Summary of Product Characteristics.
Confirm that the reprint gives a balanced/accurate view of the available information.	
Confirm that the reprint is not misleading.	Refer to Basic Principles: Exaggerated, false or misleading claims.
Has the paper been published in a peer-reviewed journal/independently refereed?	If not peer-reviewed it it must not be provided proactively.
Must prescribing information be supplied with the reprint. Does this need to be an integral part of the paper or can it/must it be given separately?	Only peer reviewed papers can be provided pro actively and the 2019 Code requires prescribing information to be provided when a reprint is provided proactively, this can be in a separate document.

Table 6: Planning promotional materials for booths at national congresses and meetings

ACTION/CHECKLIST	REFERENCE IN BOOK/CHECKLIST
Is the product or indication licensed in the UK?	Check with regulatory department or Summary of Product Characteristics for the UK.
If not, it is forbidden to promote unlicensed products or indications.	The promotion of off-label uses and unlicensed indications is not allowed in the UK at national meetings.
Do the materials have to be pre-approved by the MHRA?	This is required in certain circumstances for new products and indications (consult MHRA Blue Guide[3]).
If licensed, are all claims consistent with the licence?	Check with company regulatory department or Summary of Product Characteristics.
Are the claims accurate, balanced, based on up-to-date information, capable of substantiation?	Refer to Basic Principles: Substantiation.
Data on file is to be used as reference.	Ensure 'job bag' contains the referenced data on file in a format that has been approved ready to be supplied if requested.
If planning to use the word 'new' check this is still appropriate.	Can only be used for 12 months after a product is launched in the UK.
Check that hanging comparatives and superlatives are not being used.	Refer to Basic Principles: Comparison and hanging comparatives; Superlatives and exaggerated claims.
Check that quotes are being used correctly.	Refer to Basic Principles: Quotes.
Check that artwork such as graphs, statistics are not misleading.	Refer to Basic Principles: Artwork.
The ABPI Code requires promotional items to be certified and be allocated a unique number which should appear on promotional items.	Confirm that this is on the materials so that it can be verified as the item that has been approved. (Refer to Basic Principles: Reference Number)
Is a warning symbol required, e.g. black triangle for adverse events?	Check with company regulatory/pharmacovigilance department. (Refer to Basic Principles: Adverse Events)
Is information on how to report adverse events clearly stated?	The ABPI Code mandated wording must appear. (Refer to Basic Principles: Mandatory Warning)
Is prescribing information required on the booth panel?	This is not required for booth panels but a statement is required as to where it can be found. However it is required on all other printed promotional items, e.g. detail aids used on the booth. Refer to Chapter 3: Printed Materials and Chapter 7: Digital Media for electronic materials.

CHAPTER 3

Printed Materials

Main clauses: 4, 5, 6, 7, 8, 9, 11

Printed materials may be either promotional advertising materials or non-promotional materials, for example educational materials. There are many different types of printed advertising materials and the requirements vary according to the type of piece and the intended audience. The basic principles and procedures apply to printed materials. See Chapter 1: Basic Principles for more details.

The specific requirements for the following types of advertisements are summarised in Table 8, pages 56–61:

- ▶ Journal advertisements for UK and international audiences;
- ▶ Abbreviated advertisements;
- ▶ Loose inserts and flyers;
- ▶ Advertisements bound in and on to journals;
- ▶ Advertisements on bands and wrappers;
- ▶ Bookmarks - attached and not attached;
- ▶ Advertorials.

Table 9, pages 62–65 summarises the requirements for the following sales aids and mailings:

- ▶ Detail aids, leave pieces, mailings and flyers;
- ▶ Promotional and non-promotional letters;
- ▶ Envelopes and reply paid cards.

Table 10, page 66–69 summarises the requirements for the following materials used at meetings:

- ▶ Meeting invitations, programme, agenda, notes and lecture reports;
- ▶ Booth panels;
- ▶ Product monographs;
- ▶ Formulary packs.

Hints & Tips
Put in place a foolproof mechanism that ensures that your 'master version' of the abbreviated prescribing information, etc. is updated when changes are made to the PI, cost, etc. Ensure that your agencies always use the latest version – and double check that they have done this.

N.B. Product monographs and formulary packs are used in many situations and not just at meetings but the requirements listed in **Table 10** still apply.

This chapter has been designed to facilitate the production of printed materials. By using the tables below, quick checks can be made to decide whether printed material meets the requirements of the ABPI Code. Therefore, when producing an item of printed material, the checklist in **Table 7** should be considered PLUS specific requirements for each type of printed promotional material as summarised in **Tables 8, 9 or 10**. These tables mention, wherever possible, the main clauses that apply. However, please bear in mind that in many cases numerous clauses will apply.

Distribution of material   Clause 11

Material (including journal adverts) must only be sent or distributed to appropriate people, i.e. those who can reasonably be assumed to have a need for it. For example:

- ▶ Promotional material or advertisements for products licensed only for adults would not be suitable for paediatric journals or as mailings to be sent to paediatricians. This could be interpreted as promotion outside of the terms of the product licence; or
- ▶ Material designed for HCPs may not be suitable for administrative staff.

It is important that mailing lists correctly and appropriately categorise recipients of any mailing.

Route of distribution

Promotional material can be delivered in numerous ways:

- ▶ Via a sales representative, e.g. during a sales visit or from a booth at a meeting;
- ▶ In a journal (either as a flyer or as an advertisement on a page of the journal);
- ▶ Through the post.

The routes which MUST NOT be used for the delivery of promotional material (unless the recipient has given their permission) are mainly electronic (for more information refer to **Chapter 7: Digital Media**).

Learning from a Case: Auth/2698/1/14 – Declaration of sponsorship on promotional item
The company had certified and printed promotional materials prior to receiving feedback from the MHRA in the pre-vetting procedure. The panel considered that the impression given by the design of the front cover was such as to lead the reader to believe that this was a consensus from an independent body rather than from a company advisory panel. The panel considered that the declaration was not sufficiently prominent, nor did it accurately reflect the true involvement of the company. The panel also considered that this was disguised promotion. Consequently a breaches of clauses 9.1, 9.10 & 12.1 were ruled.
Learning Points:
- Do not proceed with production of an item in pre-vetting until all comments have been received from MHRA and have been addressed.
- The wording of the declaration of sponsorship must be unambiguous so that readers would immediately understand the extent of the company's involvement and influence over the material.

Table 7: Checklist of key issues when producing printed promotional materials

CHECKLIST OF CONTENT	ADVICE, HINTS AND TIPS
At the concept stage confirm that proposed visuals are acceptable, i.e. that they are professional, in good taste and not likely to offend. Also check whether the visual itself represents or implies a claim, e.g. age of patient or therapeutic benefit. [Clause 9]	*Refer to Basic Principles: Good taste and suitability.*
Ensure that claims are consistent with the MA.	*Refer to Basic Principles: Consistency with the marketing authorisation.*
Do the materials have to be pre-approved?	*It is a requirement in the UK that advertising for new products is approved by the MHRA.* *If the materials are to be used in other European countries (e.g. on booths at international congresses) pre-approval may be required, check with the local operating company/affiliate.*
Are the claims accurate, balanced, based on up-to-date information, capable of substantiation? [Clause 7]	*Refer to Basic Principles: Substantiation.*
If market research is to be undertaken confirm that this is conducted according to the Code. [Clause 12]	*Refer to Chapter 8. Also, if intending to carry out market research in other countries, confirm with local operating company/affiliate whether it is allowed.*
Confirm that the references substantiate the claims. [Clause 7]	*If data on file is being used, (refer to Chapter 1 page 25) it is good practice to include this in the approval folder prepared in a format so that it could be provided if requested. If intending to use data on file in another European country (e.g. on booths at international congresses) check with local operating company/affiliate if this is allowed.*
If planning to use the word 'new' confirm that it can still be used for the duration of the use of the printed materials.	*'New' can only be used in the UK for a period of 12 months after the product has been launched.*
Check that hanging comparatives, superlatives or exaggerated claims are not being used. [Clause 7]	*Refer to Basic Principles: Comparison and hanging comparatives; Basic Principles: Superlatives and exaggerated claims.*
Check that artwork, such as graphs and statistics are not misleading. [Clause 7]	*Refer to Basic Principles: Artwork.*
Obligatory information [Clause 4], e.g. adverse event reporting, prescribing information, date, reference number and non-proprietary name.	*Refer to Basic Principles:* • *Adverse Events* • *Prescribing Information* • *Date* • *Reference Number* • *Non-proprietary name* *for obligatory requirements for each type of printed material.*

Table 7: Checklist of key issues when producing printed promotional materials *continued*

CHECKLIST OF CONTENT	ADVICE, HINTS AND TIPS
Prescribing information (PI) [Clause 4] must normally be an integral part of printed promotional materials, with a few specific exceptions.	*Confirm that the PI contains all the required information (Basic Principles: Prescribing information).* *An exception to requirements for PI is abbreviated advertisements.*
The prescribing information must be legible [Clause 4]. Although not specified in the Code the following may aid legibility: • **lower case 'x' is no less than 1mm in height** • **lines no more than 100 characters in length, including spaces** • **sufficient space between lines** • **clear style of type** • **adequate contrast between text and background (dark print on light background is preferable)** • **bold headings and start each section on new line**	**Hints & Tips** **Use Table 7 (with a blank second column) as an aide mémoire in copy approval folders.**
Location of the PI: **If the PI appears overleaf in a printed journal advertisement, a reference to where it can be found must appear on the outer edge of the other page of the advert.** • **In these cases a type font of lower case 'x' no less than 2mm in height should be used**	*Confirm that the PI contains all the required information (Basic Principles: Prescribing information).*

Learning from a Case: Auth/2610/6/13 – Disguised promotion

A pharmaceutical company complained that the promotion of a competitor's product in a journal supplement in the British Journal of Clinical Pharmacy (BJPC) was disguised and that the font size of the declaration of sponsorship was disproportionately small. The supplement looked like a non-promotional educational update produced by two independent health professionals and was formatted in the style of the BJPC.

The panel noted that the company commissioning the supplement had provided the data and reviewed and approved the article. They also noted that the piece contained promotional elements and had been labelled as an 'Educational Update'. The panel ruled this was disguised promotion and a breach of clause 12.1. Additionally because the declaration of sponsorship was not sufficiently prominent a breach of clause 9.10 was ruled.

Learning Point:
• It must be readily apparent to readers if materials are promotional; they must not be disguised as independent education. Declarations of sponsorship must be prominent.

Table 8: Printed promotional materials: summary of requirements for advertisements

	CONTENT	OBLIGATORY INFORMATION	SPECIFIC REQUIREMENTS	CIRCULATION AND DISTRIBUTION
UK JOURNAL ADVERTISEMENT [Clauses 4–6]	Consider all items in Checklist of Key issues Table 7 page 54. PLUS If the advertising material appears over more than one page ensure that the individual pages are not misleading if viewed alone. 2-page advertisements that have other material in between must be treated as individual advertisements, i.e. each page requires prescribing information (PI), e.g. a 2-page advertisement on consecutive left or right hand pages, whereas 2 pages facing each other need PI on only 1 page.	Date is not required in a professional publication. The following is required: • Non-proprietary name – ensure correct size and position† • Reference number • Prescribing information** • Black triangle (if required). Refer to page 4 for minimum size requirements • Adverse event reporting prominent mandatory wording*	It must be clear that the item is an advertisement. Several formats; if advertisement is to appear in several sizes or formats each layout must be certified in its final form. Ensure the PI is legible. Page limits; no more than two pages of advertising for a product are allowed per issue of a journal. This includes loose inserts, bound in/on inserts, bands and wrappers. A summary of product characteristics is permitted as an insert in addition to the two pages of advertising.	The circulation and distribution of the journal must be appropriate for the licence of the product (refer to Distribution of material page 53). Professional publications are those sent or delivered wholly or mainly to HCPs and/or other relevant decision makers.
INTERNATIONAL JOURNAL ADVERTISEMENT [Clause 1.1]	The ABPI Code applies to all journals: • Produced in the UK in English and/or with a UK circulation even if this is only a small proportion of the overall circulation. Identification of the country of production is based on where it is compiled, edited, typeset, printed and bound, rather than on the location of the head office of the publisher • Intended for the UK wherever they are produced If the journal is covered by the scope of the Code then all the requirements for advertising must comply with the UK Code. The ABPI Code does not apply to **international** journals produced in the UK, if they are intended SOLELY for distribution outside of the UK. Note that other codes and/or regulations will apply, e.g. the IFPMA code outlines minimum global standards. MHRA guidance states UK legislation applies if journal is intended primarily for UK distribution, whether in English OR NOT.			

	CONTENT	OBLIGATORY INFORMATION	SPECIFIC REQUIREMENTS	CIRCULATION AND DISTRIBUTION
ABBREVIATED ADVERTISEMENT [Clause 5] Exempt from requirement to include PI	*Consider all items in Checklist of Key issues Table 7 page 54.* Plus when considering artwork ensure it does not convey any information not allowed in an abbreviated advertisement. Pack shots may be a problem, e.g. if they include prohibited information such as pack size.	*The following is required:* • *Name of medicine (brand or non-proprietary)* • *Non-proprietary name – ensure correct size and position[†]* • *At least one indication* • *Legal classification* • *Reference number* • *Black triangle of correct size (if required). Refer to page 4 for minimum size requirements* • *Any warning required by licensing authority* • *Name and address of MAH* • *Adverse event reporting prominent mandatory wording[*]* • *The statement "Information about this product, including adverse reactions, precautions, contraindications and method of use can be found at [the address of the website §][" and reminder to consult the SPC*	*Must not be larger than 420cm[2] (NB if it is the only advertisement on a page it is considered to be the size of the page not just the size of the advertisement that is measured).* *Must NOT include:* • *MA Number* • *Any references* • *Dosing details[‡]* • *Cost[‡]* • *Pack sizes[‡]* *MAY include:* • *Telephone numbers* • *Brief statement of reason the medicine is recommended* *Abbreviated advertisements:* • *Are NOT ALLOWED in audio-visual material, interactive data systems or on the internet even in electronic journals* • *Cannot be a loose insert or flyer* • *Cannot form part of another promotional item*	*May ONLY appear in professional publications.* **§** The website must contain the prescribing information[**]. The non-proprietary name of the medicine or list of active ingredients must appear immediately adjacent to the most prominent display of the brand name, this must be readily readable. Information about cost need not be included on the website if the advertisement only appears in journals printed in the UK which have more than 15% of their circulation outside the UK.

[*] Mandatory wording – use exact wording: refer to page 3.
[**] Prescribing information: refer to page 19 for requirements.
[†] Non-proprietary name: refer to page 18 for requirements.
[‡] Except when this is the reason the medicine is recommended.

Table 8: Printed promotional materials: summary of requirements for advertisements *continued*

	CONTENT	OBLIGATORY INFORMATION	SPECIFIC REQUIREMENTS	CIRCULATION AND DISTRIBUTION
LOOSE INSERT/FLYER [Clauses 4–6] **For distribution in a journal**	Consider all items in Checklist of Key issues Table 7 page 54. N.B. It CANNOT be an abbreviated advertisement and must be considered as a stand-alone promotional item.	The following is required: • Non-proprietary name – ensure correct size and position† • Date • Reference number • Prescribing information** • Black triangle (if required). Refer to page 4 for minimum size requirements • Adverse event reporting prominent mandatory wording*	It must be clear that the item is an advertisement. The insert cannot be larger than the page size of the journal and may not consist of more than 1 sheet per product. If printed on both sides counts as 2 pages. Page limits; no more than 2 pages of advertising for a product are allowed per issue of a journal including loose inserts. A summary of product characteristics is permitted as an insert in addition to the two pages of advertising.	The circulation and distribution of the journal must be appropriate for the licence of the product (refer to Distribution of material page 53).
BOUND-IN ADVERTISEMENT [Clause 5]	Consider all items in Checklist of Key issues Table 7 page 54. It MAY be an abbreviated advertisement; in this case follow details on page 57.	The following are required: • Non-proprietary name – ensure correct size and position† • Date (not required in professional publication) • Reference number • Prescribing information** • Black triangle (if required). Refer to page 4 for minimum size requirements • Adverse event reporting prominent mandatory wording*	It must be clear that the item is an advertisement. Bound inserts count towards the page limits of no more than 2 pages of advertising for a product per issue of a journal. A summary of product characteristics is permitted as an insert in addition to the two pages of advertising.	The circulation and distribution of the journal must be appropriate for the licence of the product (refer to Distribution of material page 53).

	CONTENT	OBLIGATORY INFORMATION	SPECIFIC REQUIREMENTS	CIRCULATION AND DISTRIBUTION
BOUND-ON ADVERTISEMENT [Clauses 4–5]	Consider all items in Checklist of Key issues Table 7 page 54. It MAY be an abbreviated advertisement; in this case follow details on page 55.	The following are required: • Non-proprietary name – ensure correct size and position† • Date (not required in professional publication) • Reference number • Prescribing information** • Black triangle (if required). Refer to page 4 for minimum size requirements • Adverse event reporting prominent mandatory wording*	It must be clear that the item is an advertisement. Bound-on advertisements count towards the page limits of no more than two pages of advertising for a product per issue of a journal. A summary of product characteristics is permitted as an insert in addition to the two pages of advertising. It cannot be larger than the size of the journal.	The circulation and distribution of the journal must be appropriate for the licence of the product. The bound-on advertisement should not be visible to the general public, e.g. the postman, and therefore it must be ensured that the wrapper for the journal is opaque.
ADVERTISING BAND AND WRAPPER [Clauses 4–6]	Consider all items in Checklist of Key issues Table 7 page 54. It CANNOT be an abbreviated advertisement and must be considered as a stand-alone promotional item.	The following are required: • Non-proprietary name – ensure correct size and position† • Date • Reference number • Prescribing information** • Black triangle (if required). Refer to page 4 for minimum size requirements • Adverse event reporting prominent mandatory wording*	Bands and wrapper advertisements count towards the page limits of no more than 2 pages of advertising for a product per issue of a journal. A summary of product characteristics is permitted as an insert in addition to the two pages of advertising. It cannot be larger than the page size of the journal.	The circulation and distribution of the journal must be appropriate for the licence of the product. The wrapper/band advertisement should not be visible to the general public, e.g. the postman, and therefore it must be ensured that the wrapper for the journal is opaque.

Hints & Tips
DVDs are professional publications and abbreviated advertisements CAN appear on the packaging.
N.B. Abbreviated advertisements are not allowed on the audio-visual material itself.

* Mandatory wording – use exact wording: refer to page 3.
** Prescribing information: refer to page 19 for requirements.
† Non-proprietary name: refer to page 18 for requirements.
‡ Except when this is the reason the medicine is recommended.

Table 8: Printed promotional materials: summary of requirements for advertisements *continued*

	CONTENT	OBLIGATORY INFORMATION	SPECIFIC REQUIREMENTS	CIRCULATION AND DISTRIBUTION
BOOKMARK (Physically attached to publication) [Clause 5]	Consider all items in Checklist of Key issues Table 7 page 54. It MAY be an abbreviated advertisement. Follow requirements for abbreviated advertisement page 57.	Is considered an integral part of the journal and therefore does not require a date IF it is a professional publication. Otherwise follow requirements for bound-in journal advertisements page 58.	Bookmarks count towards the page limits of no more than 2 pages of advertising for a product per issue of a journal. Therefore, A summary of product characteristics is permitted as an insert in addition to the two pages of advertising.	The circulation and distribution of the journal must be appropriate for the licence of the product.
BOOKMARK (NOT physically attached to publication) [Clauses 4–6]	Consider all items in Checklist of Key issues Table 7 page 54. It CANNOT be an abbreviated advertisement and must be considered as a stand-alone promotional item.	The following are required: • Non-proprietary name – ensure correct size and position† • Date • Reference number • Prescribing information** • Black triangle (if required). Refer to page 4 for minimum size requirements • Adverse event reporting prominent mandatory wording*	Bookmarks count towards the page limit of no more than 2 pages of advertising for a product per issue of a journal. Therefore, A summary of product characteristics is permitted as an insert in addition to the two pages of advertising.	The circulation and distribution of the journal must be appropriate for the licence of the product.

Hints & Tips
Inserts and supplements to print journals which are not advertisements (even though they may be promotional e.g. reports of conference proceedings), are not subject to the restrictions of Clauses 6.1 and 6.3.

	CONTENT	OBLIGATORY INFORMATION	SPECIFIC REQUIREMENTS	CIRCULATION AND DISTRIBUTION
ADVERTORIAL [Clauses 4–6]	Consider all items in Checklist of Key issues Table 7 page 54. These are promotional rather than being independent. The company may have paid for the publication and sometimes for distribution with the journal. The article or supplement may also be considered promotion if the author has been chosen by the company or if the company has prepared the manuscript or commented on the manuscript with comments other than those of factual accuracy.	For articles that name a product all the rules of promotion apply and the following are required: • Non-proprietary name – ensure correct size and position† • Date • Reference number • Prescribing information** • Black triangle (if required). Refer to page 4 for minimum size requirements • Adverse event reporting prominent mandatory wording*	It must be clear that the item is not an independent publication and sponsorship must be clearly stated. Depending on the type of advertorial, e.g. if a product is mentioned then the page limits will apply, i.e. no more than 2 pages of advertising for a product are allowed per issue of a journal. A summary of product characteristics is permitted as an insert in addition to the two pages of advertising.	Depending on the nature of the advertorial the circulation and distribution of the journal must be appropriate for the licence of the product.

* Mandatory wording – use exact wording: refer to page 3.
** Prescribing information: refer to page 19 for requirements.
† Non-proprietary name: refer to page 18 for requirements.

Table 9: Printed promotional materials: summary of requirements for sales aids and mailings

	CONTENT	OBLIGATORY INFORMATION	SPECIFIC REQUIREMENTS	USE
DETAIL AID [Clauses 4, 7, 9]	Consider all items in Checklist of Key issues Table 7 page 54. Approve as a stand-alone item.	The following are required: • Non-proprietary name – ensure correct size and position† • Date • Reference number • Prescribing information** • Black triangle (if required). Refer to page 4 for minimum size requirements • Adverse event reporting prominent mandatory wording*	If the detail aid is in loose leaf format PI must be integral to each page.	Normally used by a sales representative as an aid to a discussion when they are talking to a healthcare professional.
LEAVE PIECE [Clauses 4, 7, 9]	Consider all items in Checklist of Key issues Table 7 page 54. Approve as a stand-alone item.	The following are required: • Non-proprietary name – ensure correct size and position† • Date • Reference number • Prescribing information** • Black triangle (if required). Refer to page 4 for minimum size requirements • Adverse event reporting prominent mandatory wording*	If the leave piece is in loose leaf format PI must be integral to each page.	Normally left behind by a sales representative at the end of a sales call with an HCP.

* Mandatory wording – use exact wording: refer to page 3.
** Prescribing information: refer to page 19 for requirements.
† Non-proprietary name: refer to page 18 for requirements.

	CONTENT	OBLIGATORY INFORMATION	SPECIFIC REQUIREMENTS	USE
MAILING/FLYER [Clauses 4, 7, 9]	Consider all items in Checklist of Key issues Table 7 page 54.	The following are required: • Non-proprietary name – ensure correct size and position† • Date • Reference number • Prescribing information** • Black triangle (if required). Refer to page 4 for minimum size requirements • Adverse event reporting prominent mandatory wording*	Likely to consist of several pieces, e.g. envelope, flyer and letter. Each must be approved separately as stand-alone items.	The style of mailings often determines their acceptability to HCPs and complaints that they are being sent too frequently is most likely where their informational content is limited.
LETTER (PROMOTIONAL) [Clauses 4, 7, 9]	Consider all items in Checklist of Key issues Table 7 page 54.	The following are required: • Non-proprietary name – ensure correct size and position† • Date • Reference number • Prescribing information** (NB this must be integral to the letter, usually on the reverse) • Black triangle (if required). Refer to page 4 for minimum size requirements • Adverse event reporting prominent mandatory wording*	If a letter contains the product name and a claim (even reference to a licensed indication) it is promotional. The obligatory date can appear in the usual way for a letter.	All letters from sales staff that include a product name are normally considered promotional.

Hints & Tips

Prepare an electronic 'master version' of text with dated prescribing information and related information that must be provided in advertisements, brochures, etc. This can be provided to agencies for them to prepare promotional material.

Table 9: Printed promotional materials: summary of requirements for sales aids and mailings *continued*

	CONTENT	OBLIGATORY INFORMATION	SPECIFIC REQUIREMENTS	USE
LETTER (NON-PROMOTIONAL)		*None: provided it is non-promotional.*	*None: provided it is non-promotional.*	*Examples of non-promotional letter are:* • *Announcements of pack and price changes* • *Warning letters for adverse events provided they do not make any product claims and are accurate and factual* • *Letters written in response to an unsolicited individual enquiry, e.g. medical information letters (Refer to page 90 Reactive information)* • *Letters of response in professional journals must be accurate and factual and not be promotional*
ENVELOPE [Clause 9]	*The envelope should not bear the product brand or generic name as the envelope may be seen by a member of the public and so might be classed as advertising a POM to the public.* *The envelope may display information regarding a product's use, it must be professional, in good taste and not likely to offend the recipient or members of the public who may see it.* *It should not be misleading with respect to the contents.*	*The following are required:* • *Date of preparation* • *Reference number* • *A return address so it is clear it is from a pharmaceutical company.*	*It must be clear that the contents of the envelope are promotional.* *Therefore **DO NOT*** • *Use wording such as 'Important information/ documents enclosed – open immediately' or other such wording which may imply that the contents are about drug safety information* • *Use simulated handwritten envelopes giving a false impression that the contents are of a personal nature, e.g. a birthday card*	*To contain promotional and non-promotional materials*

	CONTENT	OBLIGATORY INFORMATION	SPECIFIC REQUIREMENTS	USE
REPLY PAID CARD **[Clause 9.8 suppl. Inf.]**	Reply paid cards may bear the name of a product (brand or generic name) or information about its usage but not both. Care must still be taken not to promote to the general public. It must be professional, in good taste and not likely to offend the recipient or members of the public who may see it.	The following are required: • Date • Reference number • Black triangle (if required). Refer to Page 4 for minimum size requirements • Adverse event reporting prominent mandatory wording*	If the RPC concerns the delivery of an item by a representative it is important that this is not an inducement to grant an interview. Therefore it should EITHER be made clear that the receipt of the item in no way depends on the representative being granted an interview OR an alternative means of delivery should be provided.	If the RPC refers to an offer of medical educational goods or services, then there must not be a link to promotion, e.g. MUST NOT be delivered with a promotional mailing.

* Mandatory wording – use exact wording: refer to page 3.
** Prescribing information: refer to page 19 for requirements.
† Non-proprietary name: refer to page 18 for requirements.

Learning from a Case: Auth/2727/8/14 – Promotion

A complaint was made that a letter sent to pharmacists did not contain required obligatory information and was inconsistent with the SPC. The company maintained the letter was a non promotional 'safety letter'. 'Safety letters' per se are not exempt from the Code and the panel noted that the letter did not appear to meet any of the listed exemptions to the definition of promotion. Overall the Panel considered that the letter was promotional and consequently ruled several breaches of the Code.

Learning Points:
- Safety letters are not exempt from being considered promotional.
- It is good practice to err on the side of caution with the interpretation of what is promotional.
- Ensure all obligatory information is included in promotional items and that they are consistent with the SPC.

Table 10: Printed promotional materials: summary of requirements for materials used at meetings

	CONTENT	OBLIGATORY INFORMATION	SPECIFIC REQUIREMENTS
MEETING INVITATION **[Clauses 4,7,9]**	Consider all items in Checklist of Key issues Table 7 page 54 and see Chapter 2. Most important, consider the IMPRESSION and the requirements of the codes concerning educational content and hospitality. The cost of hospitality must not be lavish and extravagant • Do not use terms such as 'Gala dinner' (which suggests a lavish meeting) • Do not include information and photographs from the venue or location which highlight its specific attractions • Do not suggest that a reason for attendance is local tourist opportunities	The following are required if it is promotional (i.e. contains a product name and a claim): • Non-proprietary name – ensure correct size and position† • Date • Reference number • Prescribing information** • Black triangle (if required). Refer to page 4 for minimum size requirements • Adverse event reporting prominent mandatory wording*	If an invitation contains the product name and a claim (even a reference to a licensed indication) it is promotional and it must be consistent with the SPC and contain the obligatory information. Promotional titles are best avoided in case invitations and other materials might amount to promotion. Company sponsorship must be made clear on the invitation.

Learning from a Case: Auth/2130/6/08 - Omission of PI
An advertisement for a product also mentioned another of the company's products (approved name only). A breach was ruled because no prescribing information for the second product was provided.
Learning Point:
• Include PI for all of your own products mentioned in promotional items even if you make no claims about them.

* Mandatory wording – use exact wording: refer to page 3.
** Prescribing information: refer to page 19 for requirements.
† Non-proprietary name: refer to page 18 for requirements.

MEETING PROGRAMME/AGENDA [Clauses 4, 7, 9]	CONTENT	OBLIGATORY INFORMATION	SPECIFIC REQUIREMENTS
	Consider all items in Checklist of Key issues Table 7 page 54. Most important, consider the IMPRESSION and the requirements of the codes concerning educational content and hospitality. • The cost of hospitality must not be lavish and extravagant (do not mention Gala dinner which suggests a lavish meeting) • Do not include information and photographs from the venue which highlight its specific attractions (For more information refer to Chapter 2: Meetings and Congresses.) NB the entire programme must be consistent with the SPC.	If a programme contains the product name and a claim (even reference to a licensed indication) it is promotional. The following are required if it is promotional: • Non-proprietary name – ensure correct size and position† • Date • Reference number • Prescribing information** • Black triangle (if required). Refer to page 4 for minimum size requirements • Adverse event reporting prominent mandatory wording* If non-promotional only the code number and date are required.	If a programme contains the product name and a claim (even reference to a licensed indication) it is promotional. Company sponsorship must be made clear on the invitation.

Learning from a Case: Auth/2704/3/14 – Misleading journal advertisement

A journal advertisement quoted 'current guidance' which the complainant alleged was misleading, because most practitioners would assume this was NICE guidance, which was not so for the advertisement. The Panel concluded that the impression given was that 'current guidance' implied NICE guidelines, which was not the case. Consequently a breach of clause 7.2 was ruled.

Learning Points:

• Make sure if guidelines are referenced then the body issuing the guidelines is clearly stated. (i.e. do not just reference the publication).

• Also if these guidelines have in any way been funded directly or indirectly by a marketing authorisation holder, this should be clearly stated in the promotional piece even if this was via an unrestricted educational grant.

Table 10: Printed promotional materials: summary of requirements for materials used at meetings *continued*

	CONTENT	OBLIGATORY INFORMATION	SPECIFIC REQUIREMENTS
MEETING NOTES/LECTURE REPORT [Clause 4,7,9] (see specific requirements for exceptions)	Consider all items in Checklist of Key issues Table 7 page 54. The company is responsible for notes/reports that are issued on their behalf whether produced internally or externally by speakers or other third parties. If they are promotional they must be approved and certified to ensure they meet the requirements for promotional materials.	If it contains the product name and a claim (even reference to a licensed indication), it is promotional. The following are required if it is promotional: • Non-proprietary name – ensure correct size and position† • Date • Reference number • Prescribing information** • Black triangle (if required). Refer to page 4 for minimum size requirements • Adverse event reporting prominent mandatory wording* If non-promotional only the code number and date are required.	The notes/report must be consistent with the SPC. An exception may be at a symposium held at an international congress during the research and development of a product or indication, where it might be considered a legitimate exchange of scientific information. Company sponsorship must be made clear on the lecture notes/meeting report.
BOOTH PANEL [Clause 4,7,9]	Consider Checklists Table 4 page 49 for international congresses, Table 6 page 51 for national congresses and meetings	The following are required: • Non-proprietary name – ensure correct size and position† • Date • Reference number • Prescribing information** - either on panel or statement 'PI is available at this booth' • Black triangle (if required). Refer to page 4 for minimum size requirements • Adverse event reporting prominent mandatory wording*	Refer to Chapter 2: Meetings and Congresses plus check that size of final panel will not change emphasis or balance of messages. Check requirements with LOC if panels are for an international congress.

	CONTENT	OBLIGATORY INFORMATION	SPECIFIC REQUIREMENTS
PRODUCT MONOGRAPH **[Clause 4, 7, 9]**	Consider all items in Checklist of Key issues Table 7 page 54.	The following are required: • Non-proprietary name – ensure correct size and position† • Date • Reference number • Prescribing information** • Black triangle (if required). Refer to page 4 for minimum size requirements • Adverse event reporting prominent mandatory wording*	
FORMULARY PACK [Clause 4, 7, 9]	Consider all items in Checklist of Key issues Table 7 page 54. These often consist of several items: A summary of information and letter, a product monograph, SPC, etc. all packaged together in a folder.	The following are required: • Non-proprietary name – ensure correct size and position† • Date • Reference number • Prescribing information** • Black triangle (if required). Refer to page 4 for minimum size requirements • Adverse event reporting prominent mandatory wording*	Consider each item within the pack as a stand-alone piece and then the whole folder must be approved for use together.

* Mandatory wording – use exact wording: refer to page 3.
** Prescribing information: refer to page 19 for requirements.
† Non-proprietary name: refer to page 18 for requirements.

CHAPTER 4

Public Relations

Main clauses: 7, 14, 19, 23, 25, 26, 27

A broad range of communications and activities falls under the description 'Public Relations' (PR). Press releases are perhaps the most common activity but other material such as background briefing papers, audio and video material (such as Video News Releases (VNRs) and video clips for use in news or documentary TV stories (B-rolls)) and material placed on the internet, e.g. in internet news services, must also be reviewed.

Public Relations is recognised by the Code as 'legitimate business activity' and these activities do not need formal certification but should be examined to ensure compliance. In order for PR to be a legitimate business activity, it must meet certain requirements:

► It must be non-promotional;
► The information must be 'news'. **N.B.** Information can only be news once and recycling information presented in different ways will be considered as promotion;
► The decision to contact the media proactively by issuing a media release implies that the information contained is of some significance and is newsworthy, i.e. the company must be able to justify why the information is important for the audience

Learning from a Case: Auth/2404/5/11 – Press release
A GP complained about several articles which appeared in the lay press, it was claimed that the articles contained exaggerated claims about unlicensed indications of the product which had arisen from misleading press releases issued by the MA holder. The articles contained quotations from UK experts and patient group representatives who were engaged and possibly briefed by the MA holder. It was ruled that the Company had approved this unlicensed promotion of the product.
Learning Point:
• The company is responsible for any third parties engaged on their behalf and careful briefing of spokespersons is essential, backed by written contracts/ briefings. This should include the necessity to avoid promotion to the public of prescription medicines. Press releases must not promote unlicensed uses.

at the time of its presentation. If this were not the case then the release could be considered misleading. In any case inappropriately high levels of media contact will inevitably devalue the worth of releases in the eyes of the recipients.

Provided the above requirements are met, PR departments may present information on unlicensed products and indications. This information can be presented to the general public (although the requirements for how this may be achieved will vary according to the type of audience, e.g. lay or business).

Press releases and external communications

The ABPI Code identifies press releases as a type of material that is not intended as promotional and which must be 'examined' for compliance with the Code and regulations. Companies would be well advised to include the review of media material in their Standard Operating Procedures to ensure proper 'examination'. In most situations press releases and other media material can be treated in a very similar way to promotional material with final sign-off by the 'nominated signatory'. Press releases prepared exclusively for the medical press concerning licensed products and uses could be promotional as they may not meet the requirements of being 'news' or 'newsworthy' and are likely to require formal certification by the 'nominated signatory'.

Press releases from pharmaceutical companies are usually concerned with a product or a therapeutic area in which the company has an interest. An important decision will be whether the communication is, in effect, an advertisement for the product. Several considerations will contribute to this decision and signatories should attempt to stand back and make an objective assessment of the text and underlying purpose – given its distribution and intended audience.

There have been examples of the use of inappropriate language in press releases in an attempt to capture the attention of journalists that have led to Code breaches. Restraint and objectivity are needed in press releases as with other communications about the company's prescription medicines.

One practical challenge can be that press releases may have to be produced and approved to a very tight schedule when trial results become available or a presentation is made a very short time before the press release must be distributed. Even so the company often has prior knowledge of the clinical trial that will lead to a press release, or can anticipate possible outcomes; so that much can be prepared in advance and last-minute discussions on the content of press releases can be limited to a final check.

Intended audience

Media material produced or sponsored by companies can cover a variety of topics including information on a specific medicine, significant

Hints & Tips
Identify the intended audience prominently at the top of press releases. Remember that standard wording on printed press release paper may be lost in electronic transmissions so include the intended audience at the head of the 'body copy'.

research developments, general disease information and information not specifically related to the company's products, such as general business information. Press releases and related media material can be conveniently divided into three categories according to their intended audience:

Hints & Tips
Prepare draft press releases ahead of time by, for example, anticipating possible outcomes from clinical trials. The content should then just require a final check.

> ▶ Lay press;
> ▶ Business press; and
> ▶ Medical press.

Whilst it is possible to produce one press release for two, or even all three audiences, it is usually easier and more appropriate to produce separate releases. This is because the Code is likely to judge press releases according to their intended audience and therefore by different criteria.

A news item that justifies a medical press release may not be suitable as the basis for a lay press release and it may not have a business angle that justifies a business release. A press release directed at the public must be extremely careful not to constitute promotion of a prescription-only medicine. For business information the Code recognises that Stock Exchange rules require that important new information on development and marketed medicines is made available to investors. This means that in practice the availability of results from an important clinical trial could lead to two or three press releases written in quite different ways:

> ▶ A lay press release that is scrupulously non-promotional and probably orientated to the disease area;
> ▶ A business release that identifies the importance of the results from a business perspective (e.g. supporting an application for a licence in a new, large market); and
> ▶ A medical release that is orientated to the medical news value of the results.

Each press release should identify the intended audience and only be sent to appropriate outlets for that audience; for example a business release should be directed at financial publications and financial correspondents. Identifying the nationality (or international nature) of the intended audience is also advisable because many press releases find their way onto the internet and are copied by several news agencies. To have identified clearly that the communication is, for example 'For the UK medical press' can be a useful defence if an article appears in another country, e.g. the USA, where the regulations, and quite possibly the licensed uses of the product, are different.

Lay media material

N.B. Lay media includes the medical correspondents of both newspapers and magazines in addition to general correspondents.

Media material (press packs and news releases) concerning prescription-only products has many of the same requirements as materials for other audiences, i.e. it must be factual, accurate and balanced and must not mislead with respect to safety. However it must also meet the following requirements:

Learning from a Case: Auth/2273/10/09 – Public relations materials
A complaint was made about promotional and press materials issued by a pharma company to mark a product launch. These materials included a media backgrounder, a lay press release and a medical press release but did not include details of precautions or side effects.
It was alleged that the backgrounder was misleading, exaggerated and not capable of substantiation and the lay press release included very positive claims but lacked information about side effects which in effect turned the lay press release in to an advert for POMs.
An interview with an HCP briefed by the pharma company made misleading and unsubstantiated claims for the product. Breaches of the Code were ruled for both the press release and the interview.
Learning Points:
- All materials including press releases must be factual, balanced and consistent with the SPC.
- Care must be taken with lay press packs so that prescription only medicines are not advertised to the public. Materials aimed at patients must not be promotional.

> ▶ It must be non-promotional. Deciding what does and does not constitute advertising/promotion can be difficult with many items and particularly so with PR activities. The key criterion for whether a press release breaches the 'no promotion' rule is a judgement on whether it is made for the purpose of encouraging members of the public to ask their healthcare professional to prescribe a specific prescription-only medicine;

> ▶ It must not raise unfounded hopes of successful treatment, e.g. raise the hope of cures for currently incurable conditions.

It is possible to discuss products or indications in development provided this is carried out in a non-promotional manner and the information is both 'news' and 'newsworthy' (see **Press Releases** in this chapter for general information).

Lay media material should be examined for compliance with the Code but does not require formal certification. This is often carried out using the same processes used by the Company for approval of promotional materials. Although not a requirement it is wise to include a reference number and a date of dissemination for identification purposes. Lay media material does not require prescribing information but it is considered good practice to include a copy of the SPC with the materials.

Business media material

In practice media material aimed at the financial press and financial correspondents of lay publications is likely to be subject to different acceptability criteria from material directed at the medical or general pages of the lay press. The requirement by Stock Market rules to inform shareholders of significant business developments is recognised by the Code and this will be taken into consideration when deciding whether a communication constitutes promotion to the public.

Key Point
A lay press release must not be made for the purpose of encouraging members of the public to seek a prescription for a prescription-only product.

Table 11: Interactions with the media

KEY POINTS TO REMEMBER	COMMENTS
Do not use media material to promote prescription-only medicines to the public.	*The line between promotion and non-promotional material is important but is often difficult to judge. Refer to Lay Media Material.*
Information must be factual and balanced.	*Ignoring negative elements, e.g. warnings and adverse reactions, could mislead.*
Companies are responsible for the activities of agencies working on their behalf.	*Establish clear procedures for review and approval of agency work.*
Care is needed when responding to requests for information from journalists.	*You will be asked to provide copies of information supplied in the event of a complaint.*
Meetings for journalists must comply with the same requirements as meetings for health professionals.	*Ensure that the venue and location are appropriate. Hospitality must be subsistence only and at the level recipients would pay for themselves.*
Press releases and financial information for shareholders must be examined for compliance with the Code and regulations.	*Take into account the way in which the item will be used, e.g. how and to whom it will be distributed.*

Table 12: Is it promotion/advertising or not?

CONTRIBUTING FACTORS	COMMENTS
Use of brand names.	*Multiple use of brand names rather than generic names creates an impression of promotion.*
Apparent intent.	*The content, and the way in which it is presented, will give a good indication of whether the likely intent was to encourage prescribing.*
To whom the release was sent.	*Some information is likely to have greater relevance to one particular audience rather than another.*
Time from launch.	*A release sent several years before any product is available is less likely to be considered promotional in intent than one sent a few weeks or months pre-launch.*
Product availability.	*A release on a possible future indication for a currently available product must be particularly careful not to encourage 'off-label' use.*

The content of media material must be genuinely business orientated and distribution must be to journalists who write business stories. This can be achieved by clearly identifying the business angle of a medical development. Examples include linking the news to a regulatory submission or identifying the potential size of a new market opening.

Hints & Tips
Review of business press material from a Code viewpoint must be integrated with ensuring compliance with Stock Market rules on disclosure of material business information.

Not all companies operating in the UK are quoted on the UK Stock Exchange and, although no case reports confirm this supposition, it could be more difficult for a company without UK shareholders to justify product business PR activities in the UK. This might be a relevant consideration if a press release results in an apparently promotional newspaper story and distribution had not been restricted to business correspondents and/or the content was not clearly business orientated.

Business media material includes news stories not directly related to products and associated therapy areas. Such stories include topics such as building new production or research facilities, the appointment of new executives and staff redundancies. Such material wouldn't normally be subject to the Code unless it concerns medicines. Activities by companies and their agencies in support of, for example, generic medicines, although not promotional for any specific medicine brand, have been considered subject to the Code.

In approving any media material the nominated signatory must ensure that it is factually correct and balanced and takes into account the information needs of the target audience (Clause 7 does not apply to this type of information). Misjudgements by reviewers can lead to breaches of the Code and could also lead to costly legal action, particularly in the USA (even though the communication may have originated from elsewhere). Exaggerating the benefits, not providing appropriately balanced information on safety or being sufficiently clear about uncertainties, might be said to have misled investors and could result in large financial penalties.

Medical media material

N.B. This means materials intended for an audience of HCPs and does not include the medical columns of lay journals or newspapers.

Learning from a Case: Auth 2705/3/14 – Press release
This was a complaint about a press release which made claims based on a secondary endpoint of a study in which the primary endpoint had failed. The Panel ruled the press release misleading because it failed to put the secondary endpoint data into the context of the failed primary endpoint
Learning Points:
- Study data must be placed within the context of the primary outcome results.
- It is not acceptable to make claims and present secondary endpoint data without mentioning the primary endpoint results with similar emphasis.
- The fairness and balance of product-related content in press releases will be assessed against similar criteria to promotional material.

Even though media materials must be non-promotional, all the usual quality of information criteria that would apply to a promotional item should be considered. (Refer to **Table 7: Checklist of key issues when producing printed promotional materials** page 54.) However press releases usually concentrate on a narrow topic such as the results from a single important clinical trial. This can provide challenges when considering how to judge whether the information is balanced, objective, not misleading and 'sufficiently complete to enable the recipient to form their own opinion of the therapeutic value of the medicine'. It should be possible to satisfy these requirements by including information that puts the new information fairly and objectively in the context of all the available information. So, for example, new positive results for a product in a comparison with an alternative treatment should be put into the context of any previous comparisons (especially if these were less favourable!) to avoid the danger of being misleading. Alternatively reference could be made to credible sources of information such as expert clinical guidelines from learned societies.

In a press release reporting on a single clinical trial appropriate weight should be given to different aspects of the study. The press release should not report only positive efficacy findings while neglecting to mention the side effects reported. The uncertain nature of the information should be acknowledged as safety and efficacy have not been established for unlicensed or off-label uses.

It is acceptable to discuss products or indications in development provided this is carried out in a non-promotional manner and the information is both 'news' and 'newsworthy' (See Press Releases in this chapter) but care is needed to ensure it is not, in reality, advertising. Several factors are likely to be considered in adjudicating this aspect (Refer **Table 12: Is it promotion/ advertising or not?** page 74) but no one factor can be said to be a sole determinant. The licence status of the product should be made clear, this is particularly important if the product is not licensed or the media release refers to an unlicensed indication.

Medical media material should be examined for compliance with the Code but does not require formal certification. This is often carried out using the same processes used by the company for approval of promotional materials. Although not a requirement it is wise to include a reference number and a date of dissemination for identification purposes. Non-promotional medical media material does not require prescribing information but it is considered good practice to include a copy of the SPC with the materials.

Use of quotations

A media communication doesn't seem complete without a quotation from a company executive, a key opinion leader or a patient. Commonly, a quotation from an eminent clinician is included in press releases commenting on the significance of the news. That quotation may reflect the clinician's view but if it is inaccurate, misleading or in some other way not compliant with the Code then the company issuing the release will be held responsible.

Quotations must be faithfully reproduced and must accurately reflect the meaning of the author. The source of the quotation must be identified.

Quotations from speakers at meetings must only be used with their formal permission. In practice it is advisable to document in some way (e.g. a letter or e-mail) that the originator has given his/her approval for the use of the quotation.

Quotations from the company chief executive or some other important company figure are also often included in media material. It is important that their contribution is subject to review to ensure code compliance.

Use of brand names

The use of brand names, rather than approved names, in media material is likely to be a factor taken into consideration in the event of media material being subject to a Code complaint that it constituted promotion of an unlicensed product or use, or promotion of a prescription product to the public. Repeated and prominent use of brand names and the use of product logos could be taken to indicate promotional intent. As a 'rule of thumb', using the brand name only once (or possibly twice including the title) alongside the approved name presents a defensible position that promotion is not intended. However the use of the brand name is only one factor amongst several that will be considered in a Code complaint. The complete avoidance of brand names does not guarantee that an item will be judged non-promotional.

Prescribing information

Although the inclusion of the Summary of Product Characteristics (SPC) in press packs is not spelt out as a requirement it does provide useful information for the recipients and inclusion is good practice. The SPC is not in itself promotional material so its inclusion shouldn't result in a non-promotional item becoming promotional. Remember that Code judgements have generally assumed that readers will not necessarily read 'the small print' so do not rely on the fact that information is in the prescribing information as a reason for not including important information in the body of a press release. For example, if there are particular precautions or restrictions on usage that are relevant to the subject of the communication, inclusion of the SPC in the press pack is unlikely to be an acceptable reason not to mention them in the body copy.

Use of patient case studies

Inclusion of a real-life case study can enhance media material, bringing a human-interest aspect and appeal to journalists. Review of patient case studies must consider several aspects from a Code perspective.

It is likely that the chosen case study will be positive for the subject medicine and care must be taken to ensure that the communication remains balanced and reflects all the available data. PMCPA advice is that the case results should be 'typical' and it would almost certainly be considered misleading to choose a

> **Hints & Tips**
> It is a helpful exercise when reviewing quotations to imagine the quotation marks are removed and ask 'Can the company justify the statement as truthful, balanced and in every way compliant with the Code?'

patient with an outstandingly positive outcome. Concentration on one, or a few, positive case reports could mislead as to the true efficacy and tolerability of a medicine. Inclusion of positive case reports in a lay press communication could cause it to, in effect, be promotion of a prescription medicine to the public.

Hints & Tips
PMCPA advice on case studies: Patients chosen must be typical in terms of their condition and response to therapy.

Companies should also consider patient confidentiality and ensure that the patient has consented to the use of his/her comments in media material. The patient should be fully aware of the uses that their contribution will be put to. Ideally this should be documented in a written agreement.

Interviews and press meetings require careful preparation and briefing to ensure compliance because the company could be held responsible for the content.

Questions are sometimes raised about payment for services provided by patients. The Code does not prohibit this and in principle there is no reason why payment should not be offered providing it represents a fair rate for the work done and time given up (and this is likely to be much less than rates offered for work by healthcare professionals). However any remuneration must not be an inducement to speak more favourably about a product. It may be appropriate to offer a fair and reasonable payment to a patient group for their efforts in identifying suitable patients to contribute to case reports but, again, it should not amount to an inducement to encourage an action favourable for the company or its product.

Press releases from third parties

Clinical research projects are often undertaken in collaboration with bodies that may wish to issue their own press releases. Independent healthcare organisations and individual healthcare professionals also may wish to makes statements or issue press material relating to your products. As long as this is undertaken in a truly independent manner then the company will not normally be held responsible for the content of their outputs. However the company may well be involved to various degrees and if the press material would breach the code in some way, a judgement will be made on whether the company should be held responsible. The independent initiators may, for example, submit their draft material for review by someone in the company (not necessarily the nominated signatories!) and a failure to advise appropriate corrections and changes could be sufficient to suggest that the company is complicit and a Code breach could be ruled.

Learning from a Case: Auth/2308/4/10 – Company involvement was not transparent
A letter to The Times newspaper concerning differences between branded and generic medicines and signed by several patient organisations and health professionals was not promotional for any medicine. However, the company had been instrumental in the development and production of the letter. It was considered subject to the Code as it was information about prescription medicines aimed at the public. The company's involvement was not made clear in the letter. The panel ruled that by not declaring its involvement in the creation of the letter the company had failed to maintain high standards
Learning Point:
* A company's PR activities concerning medicines in general, as well as specific medicines, may be subject to the Code. The company's role in PR activities must be transparent.

COMPLIANCE, CODES AND COMMUNICATIONS

Employee communications and internal PR

Employees are members of the public and companies should not promote prescription-only medicines to them. However they also have a legitimate business interest in the affairs of the company and communications about the company's products designed to keep them informed about significant developments are very unlikely to be considered as 'promotion to the public'. This is likely to extend to keeping them aware of promotional campaigns.

Hints & Tips
Ensure that your SOPs make it clear that only nominated signatories may review materials, even those produced 'independently' by third parties.

However should a company undertake an initiative that is designed to encourage employees to seek a prescription for one of its products for themselves or friends and relatives then that could result in a Code breach. The activities of company occupational health departments are best kept well separated from commercial departments.

Press conference/interview

Meetings with journalists must comply with exactly the same requirements on hospitality that apply to healthcare professional meetings. The choice of venues and the subsistence provided will be judged on the same criteria. Remember that the Code can be applied to invitations to UK journalists given from outside the UK so you should ensure that the arrangements are checked against the requirements of the ABPI Code and formal certification will be required, as for HCP meetings, if the venue is outside the UK.

The Code states that the requirements for meetings apply to journalists without identifying any exceptions. This means that journalists may not be paid for attending meetings although travel (the same conditions apply as for other delegates), accommodation and meal expenses could be covered. However, as for healthcare professionals, in some circumstances journalists are contracted to work for the company. When this is the basis for the relationship one would expect their outputs to be produced primarily for the company rather than an independent publication and be subject to review and approval before dissemination. The arrangements should be clearly set out, e.g. in a written contract.

You should not pay a journalist to attend a press briefing or attend a meeting in the expectation that they will write an article. A journalist paid by the company becomes, in effect, contracted to the company to produce something for them and the company is likely to be held responsible for his/her outputs. The Code of Practice Authority has stated that you should not pay a journalist or publication to publish an article based on a press release you have issued so care is needed if there is any financial arrangement with the publication, e.g. the company has bought advertising space. Publication of the article should not be conditional on the financial arrangement. If the company does pay a journal for publication it becomes an advertisement and

Hints & Tips
Your company is responsible for the outputs of your agencies, so ensure that review and approval requirements are included in their contracts.

this must be made readily apparent and all the requirements for advertisements must be met.

Hints & Tips
Do not pay journalists to attend press briefings; to do so means your company is likely to be held responsible for any of their outputs.

When a company sponsors a journalist to attend a meeting it is reasonable to assume that they intend that he/she writes articles based on what they hear. This will be reinforced by any material they provide to help the journalist. The company should therefore make an assessment of the likely outputs since they may be held responsible if an inappropriate output could reasonably have been expected.

Responding to enquiries

When a company is responding to an unsolicited request for information from a journalist this may cast the interaction in a slightly different light from when publicity is actively sought by, or on behalf of, the company. Nevertheless you still cannot promote a prescription-only medicine to the public, promote an unlicensed product/indication or break the Code in any other way. The response to the enquiry, like all other information, must be accurate, balanced, fair, objective and unambiguous. The information provided must reflect clearly all the evidence and must not mislead either directly or by implication, by distortion, exaggeration or undue emphasis. In practice this is likely to mean that, when a request for information on a new positive trial is received, then a response should put the new trial in context of earlier studies or any relevant important precautions.

When a TV programme or newspaper is spontaneously running a story on a product they may request a pack shot, footage of the product on a production line or similar material that depicts the product. Usually it should be acceptable to provide such material reactively.

Articles and advertorials

Some publications offer the opportunity to sponsor articles within the journal itself, in a supplement or as leaflet inserts. Various arrangements are possible including possibilities to influence the content to various degrees, directly or indirectly. The company's responsibility depends on the influence it has exerted over the content or the financial arrangements.

The company will be deemed to have had influence if any of the following apply:
- The company instigated or paid for any aspect of the article, e.g. a placement fee;
- The company or its agency wrote the article;
- The company chose the authors;
- The company chose the topic or scope of the article;
- The company provided information for the article;
- The company or its agency had editorial control over the article.

Hints & Tips
If purchase of advertising space brings the opportunity to influence the content of an adjacent article it might be considered promotion.

A key requirement is transparency. The company's involvement should be readily apparent and accurately portrayed. The following are examples:

- ▶ **A sponsored article** This is likely to require a prominent statement outlining the arrangements. This could be something like, for example, 'This article has been sponsored by X-Company who suggested possible topics and authors to the publishers';
- ▶ **An advertorial** An article paid for and written by the Company or its agency, published unaltered. This should be immediately recognisable as paid-for advertising. A prominent statement at the top of the page such as 'This is an advertisement from X-Company' would be appropriate and all the requirements of promotional materials must be met.

A sponsored article cannot be a vehicle for the company to promote off-label or undertake promotion that would not be acceptable if undertaken by the company directly. Whether a company would be judged as responsible for a sponsored article will depend on the circumstances of the case. Relevant factors will be any input the company has provided to the content, such as providing source material for the authors and the opportunity to review and comment on drafts.

Signatories are likely to be rather cautious about deciding that an item is non-promotional where there is any uncertainty. If an item is subsequently ruled to be advertising, multiple breaches of the Code may result, e.g. omission of prescribing information, promotion of unlicensed uses or products as well as disguised promotion.

Internet and newswires

The internet and other electronic communications such as newswires have become the main way that news stories reach their intended journalist audience. Media releases, and agency reports based on these releases, appear rapidly on internet sites and can be the source of media stories throughout the world. That media releases should clearly state their intended audience, is therefore particularly important if the information may be inappropriate in some way outside the originating country. Similar considerations are valid when placing press releases on internet sites including 'internet press rooms' and companies may consider requiring journalists to register their area of work so that, for example, a media release intended for a medical audience is not inadvertently directed at a lay journalist.

In addition to the well-known press agency services such as Reuters that distribute their material widely on the basis of their analysis of its newsworthiness some agencies offer a paid-for service whereby media releases are targeted at specific journalists and publications in certain countries. Although there are no Code cases to confirm this, it seems likely that these activities would be considered as if the company had sent the release directly to the journalist. A breach of the Code would therefore be possible if, say, a foreign head office subscribed to this service and sent a media release that was not compliant with the UK Code to a UK journalist.

Many companies put their press releases and additional media material onto a website or 'virtual press room'. This material will of course be available to all site visitors and it seems advisable to require registration of interested journalists according to whether they are writing for the lay, business or medical press.

Hints & Tips
Prepare a detailed written briefing document prior to media interviews to ensure that the interviewee is clear on acceptable responses. The briefing also acts as a record of the intent of the company.

Companies often have a press area within their corporate sites. This will usually come within the 'business press' category and contain stories of business and financial relevance.

Where a website contains information that is promotional (some medical press material intended for a healthcare professional audience could be considered promotional), you must also provide information for the public to avoid them having to access the material intended for health professionals. The links to material for each target audience must be clearly separated and the intended audience identified.

VNRs and B-rolls, and media interviews

Media material includes recorded audio and video material such as Video News Releases (VNRs) and video clips for use in news or documentary TV stories (B-rolls). Unless these are distributed only to specialist channels destined for viewing only by health professionals they must be non-promotional.

The broad context in which the material is provided will be relevant to Code decisions on whether the material should be classified as promotional. There may be considerable media 'noise' about a particular subject (such as a truly breakthrough treatment) that justifies a company producing balanced product related material. On the other hand producing and circulating material for TV and radio to coincide with the launch of a new product is likely to be perceived as an attempt to encourage members of the public to request the prescription medicine from their healthcare professional and therefore breach the Code and the law.

The same requirements apply to live or recorded media interviews but there is the added complication that the signatory has no chance to review and approve the final 'output'. Careful briefing of the interviewee is therefore essential and written briefing notes outlining what should and should not be said could prove useful in the event of a complaint. It is appropriate that such briefing notes are approved by the company's signatories - although this is not a Code requirement.

Remember that if interviews are recorded the production team may edit the recording and distort the balance of the item. A company is unlikely to be held responsible for distortion by journalists but if there is an important point that you determine must be made (e.g. that the product in question is not yet approved for use) your briefing for the interviewee could advise that this point is repeated whenever possible to minimise the chances that it will be edited out.

Whether the media material is produced proactively or in response to a journalist's request may be a relevant factor in judging the activity under the Code.

KOLs/spokespersons

It is important to distinguish when a KOL is acting independently or if they are acting on behalf of a company. If the latter is true, then the company is responsible for any statement made verbally or in writing.

The KOL will be considered to be acting on behalf of the company, for example if they are commissioned and paid by the company to write articles or attend media interviews or even if the company has editorial control over any outputs from such activities.

In such circumstances a consultancy agreement must be in place (See **Chapter 1: Basic Principles – Consultancy agreements and payment**), it is important that spokespersons are adequately briefed to avoid Code breaches.

Scope of company responsibility

The pharmaceutical company will be considered responsible for any activity undertaken 'with its authority', i.e. it is responsible for the activities of third parties such as public relations agencies who it engages either directly or indirectly.

A UK company is responsible for any activity directed towards a UK audience. There have been instances where European, international or global headquarters have released materials that mention the use of a product in the UK; in such circumstances the UK affiliate will be held responsible. It is, therefore, recommended that procedures are put in place to ensure that these materials are examined to ensure that they comply with the requirements of the UK Code.

However a UK company is unlikely to be held responsible for material directed by its headquarters to international media even if this is subsequently picked up by UK media.

UK companies are responsible for the materials they provide, e.g. media materials and briefings and not necessarily the end product produced by journalists. A company isn't likely to be held responsible for inaccurate reporting from journalists provided either the material provided by the company was accurate or the journalist was acting entirely on their own account (i.e. had researched the topic themselves, the company had no financial or editorial input).

Table 13: Media materials – checklist

Feel free to photocopy this page when reviewing and approving materials. Always check the Code and regulations!

ASPECT	CHECKED: ✓	COMMENTS
Intended audience identified and stated? • Medical/Lay/Business • UK/European/International		
Is the content appropriate for the intended audience?		
Distribution list appropriate?		
Is the content truly non-promotional?		
If the item is promotional does it include all required information (prescribing information, cost, etc.)?		
Appropriate use of brand v. approved names?		
Accurate and factually correct?		
Balanced?		
Reflects all the available evidence?		
Regulatory status (e.g. unlicensed use) clearly apparent?		
Quotations: • Authorised? • Accurate and accurately reflect the true meaning? • Comply with all aspects of the Code?		
Newsworthy?		
Not representing old data as new?		
Appropriate language used?		

CHAPTER 5

Information to General Public and Patients

Main clauses: 25,26,27

In the UK prescription-only medicines must not be advertised to the public. The only exceptions are vaccination campaigns that have been approved by government health ministers (in effect by the MHRA on their behalf).

Drawing a line between non-promotional information and promotion/advertising can be very difficult. The main criterion is whether the communication was made for the purpose of encouraging members of the public to ask their health professional to prescribe a specific prescription-only medicine. Although the Code refers to intent, it is likely that the effect of the communication will also be considered; after all it is a reasonable assumption that companies are, or should be, aware of the likely outcomes of their information provision activities. It is not a good defence to claim there was no intention to encourage members of the public to request a medicine if this outcome seems obvious to a well-informed observer. Make a detached judgement of how the activity would appear from a competitor's viewpoint.

Non-promotional information vs. advertising

Consider the following in any information made available to the general public:

▶ **Balance and accuracy**: ensure that the communication is factual and balanced. Consider the balance of disease information and other treatment options;

▶ **Branding**: Avoid branding or promotional appearance. Use the approved name rather than the brand name; use of the brand name is likely to be deemed promotional although in some circumstances it may be used once for identification purposes;

▶ **Language used**: Do not use emotive language when describing the product, e.g. describing the results of a study as 'stunning' or a product as a 'miracle drug'. The information must not raise unfounded hopes of successful treatment nor mislead with respect to safety. Ensure that the language used does not make it sound like an advert for the product;

► **Distribution**: The method of distribution and how recipients become aware of it are important factors. Information for the general public must apply the same high-quality criteria as that provided for health professionals.

Hints & Tips:
The interpretation by national legislators and codes of practice of what constitutes advertising to the public varies. Patient communication initiatives in one country cannot be assumed to be acceptable in other European countries and beyond. National checking is essential and it is rarely possible to run a single programme across Europe.

However, patients and the public will not generally have good medical knowledge, so something that would be perfectly acceptable for health professionals might sound confusing, ambiguous or misleading for a lay reader.

Make a detached judgement of whether the activity is non-promotional and how it would appear to others:

► Does the activity appear more like an advertisement than a medical communication?
► Are marketing or medical personnel, or both, driving the activity?
► Is the activity fulfilling a genuine information gap?
► How might a major competitor view the activity?

Categories of information to the public

Information to the public falls into three categories depending on its purpose, how it is disseminated and how the public is made aware of it. Companies must take particular care if dissemination is via social media. The three categories are as follows:

► Proactive;
► Reactive;
► Reference.

Proactive information

Mentioning a specific prescription medicine: Proactive information must not be provided if it mentions a product in a way that will or is likely to encourage members of the general public to ask their doctor to prescribe it. Mentioning a product means using either the brand or generic name and includes indirect references, e.g. referring to an oral treatment when all the other treatments are injections. The product name can be used in a context with other treatments for the condition provided that equal weight is given to the product and the other treatments and that comments are not made about the product which are likely to encourage the individual to request their doctor to prescribe it. Information should not include pack shots, this would very likely be seen as promotion.

Disease awareness information

Important types of information for patients and the public are disease awareness activities or campaigns. These constitute proactive information centred on disease awareness rather than

Hints & Tips
Disease awareness campaign materials should identify the sponsoring company but should not contain sufficient detail to identify a specific medicine.

medicines and can include several related aspects including buying advertising space in mass media.

Hint & Tips
When reviewing material it is helpful to compare why a competitor might consider the material to be promotional and you may not. Next, consider both viewpoints from an adjudicator's perspective.

The intent of the communication is likely to be to encourage patients to visit their healthcare professional or to seek further information, e.g. from a help-line, website or by post. Disease awareness campaigns may enhance the public's ability to identify disease symptoms; help to overcome embarrassment associated with some conditions or let patients know that certain medical problems can be improved by treatment if they visit their doctor.

In most situations there is no mention of medicines and often no information on treatment options. Disease awareness campaigns must not promote specific prescription medicines and, while there could be a mention of treatments in general, identification of a specific medicine by brand or non-proprietary name is likely to be seen as promoting that medicine. Even identifying a medicine indirectly, e.g. by referring to a unique feature such as 'the once-daily treatment for XX' is likely to result in a Code breach.

Describing a range of treatments could be acceptable depending on the type of communication. The key criterion of acceptability is likely to be whether the campaign would lead to a particular medicine being requested or favoured. With this in mind it could be acceptable to include a mention of the company's medicine amongst several others (and without any emphasis or favouritism) in a fairly detailed, disease-orientated booklet.

Particular care is needed when a company has the only medicine that could be used for the disease in question. In this situation, to say that the disease can be treated if the patient visits their doctor could, in effect, be promoting a specific medicine. Even so diseases that were previously untreatable may be particularly appropriate (from a patient welfare viewpoint) as subjects of disease awareness campaigns and each situation will be judged on its merits. Highlighting that there are both medical and other (e.g. surgical) treatments available may be an appropriate way to avoid promoting a specific prescription medicine in these circumstances.

It would be acceptable, in principle, to use patients or celebrities in a non-promotional disease-awareness campaign, however, responsibility for what they say, e.g. if they promote a prescription-only product, remains with the company. Very careful briefing is required, including documented instructions, to ensure that they understand the restrictions that apply. As discussed in **Chapter 4: Public Relations**, using testimonies from patients or celebrities runs the risk of being unbalanced and not representing a 'typical patient'. The MHRA has issued guidelines on disease awareness campaigns, these are available on their website.

Key Point
Is the communication made for the purpose of encouraging members of the public to ask their health professional to prescribe a specific prescription-only medicine? If so this is not acceptable.

Learning from a Case: Auth/2526/8/12 – Disease awareness campaigns
A doctor alleged that an advertisement in a lifestyle magazine was in breach of the Code.
Amongst other information the following statements appeared but in a bolder font, 'It is possible to prevent shingles' and 'See your GP who can give you more information'. Readers were then directed to other information on the shingles aware website (sponsored by a company who had recently launched a vaccine to prevent shingles) or an independent patient organization website. Readers could scan a QR Code with a smart phone to access the shingles aware website.
The Panel considered that the advertisement posed the question 'how do you prevent shingles?' and answered that question with the name of the product which was the subject of the first item on the homepage of the patient organisation website. The Panel considered that the combined effect of the advertisement and websites was to promote to the general public. A breach of the Code was ruled.
The Panel considered that the material (the advertisement and websites combined) was not balanced. There was a disproportionate emphasis on vaccination, including mentioning the name of the vaccine.
The Panel noted that whilst disease awareness was in principle a legitimate and helpful activity, caution should be exercised when there was only one product available.
Learning Point:
- Disease awareness activities must be balanced and take due account of all possible management approaches. The overall impression and 'take away messages' are important.

Information after the prescription

Leaflets and booklets may be produced for patients who have been prescribed a medicine. They can be distributed by healthcare professionals or directly to patients and may contain information on diseases or company products. As with all communications for the public they must be factual and non-promotional. The distinction that the patient has already been prescribed the medicine is an important one and several companies have set up information services that are restricted to this group. Distribution via health professionals is one way of ensuring that only patients who have been prescribed the medicine have access to the information. Examples of other ways to restrict access to these patients include setting up controlled-access websites containing information on prescription medicines where entry is controlled, e.g. by registration through their prescriber or by entering the marketing authorisation number that appears on the pack.

One potentially tricky area of information for patients who have been prescribed a medicine is the distinction between promoting therapy concordance and encouraging a patient to ask for a particular medicine. Language and tone will be a relevant consideration and also great care must be taken to ensure that information does not continue to be provided once the patients are no longer taking the medicine. Frequent 're-registration' in information schemes is advisable for long-term schemes.

Any material relating to a medicine intended for patients taking it must include the statement below or a similar one which conveys the same meaning:

> *Reporting of side effects*
> *If you get any side effects, talk to your doctor, pharmacist or nurse. This includes any possible side effects not listed in the package leaflet. You can also report side effects directly via the Yellow Card Scheme at **www.mhra.gov.uk/yellowcard**. By reporting side effects you can help provide more information on the safety of this medicine.*

When the material relates to a medicine which is subject to additional monitoring an inverted black equilateral triangle (see **Chapter 1: Basic Principles**) must be included on it together with the statement below or a similar one:

> *This medicine is subject to additional monitoring. This will allow quick identification of new safety information. You can help by reporting any side effects you may get. See www.mhra.gov.uk/yellowcard for how to report side effects.*

Business

The Code recognises that information on medicines given to business audiences must be treated somewhat differently from that directed at patients and the general public. The normal requirements and needs of running a business cannot be overridden because of the 'no promotion of prescription medicines to the public' rule. Stock Market rules require that companies make public information that could materially affect their share price. Also current and potential employees require quite extensive information about the medicines that are at the centre of business operations.

Financial information

Financial information such as annual reports and announcements about significant business news provided to inform shareholders, the Stock Exchange, business journalists, etc. will inevitably need to include information on existing medicines and indications as well as those not yet marketed. It must be factual and presented in a balanced way taking into account the information needs of the target audience. Clause 7 does not apply to financial information. Refer to **Chapter 4: Public Relations** for more information on press releases and employee communications.

Corporate advertising

Companies may decide to take advertising space in lay publications to promote their image. This may be in a newspaper, magazine, digital or broadcast media. Sometimes such advertisements are associated with articles or supplements on disease areas in which the company has an interest. These advertisements can draw attention to the company's research interests and investment commitment, etc. but in most circumstances mentioning specific medicines by brand name, approved name or description is likely to be considered as promotion of a prescription medicine, even if no promotional claims are made.

Advertisements should be reviewed and approved in the context of the publications in which they appear. Some science publications are directed at the public, rather than healthcare professionals and administrative staff, and should therefore not carry advertisements for prescription medicines.

Learning from a Case: Auth 1942/1/07 – Misleading advertisement in lay press
An advertisement in the 'Big Issue' magazine included the text: 'But the good news is with modern treatments there's now a real chance of recovery'. This was ruled misleading because lay people might assume this meant elimination of the disease.
Learning Point:
- Always consider how a lay reader without specialist knowledge might interpret the words.

Companies may produce brochures about their business; again these may not promote any prescription-only medicines to the public. The intended, and actual, audience for these brochures will be relevant when deciding what constitutes acceptable content. Items distributed only to current and potential employees or site visitors may be considered in a different light from those distributed

Hints & Tips
An easy way to include the up-to-date SPC and PIL in electronic material viewed on line is to include a prominent link direct to the document in the electronic medicines compendium www.medicines.org.uk/emc

widely to the general public. In some circumstances signatories may feel that they could defend inclusion of a simple listing of a company's products as not amounting to an advertisement for these products. However, whatever the type and circumstances of the brochure it should not encourage members of the public to ask for a particular prescription medicine.

Reactive information

This is essentially the company's medical information service, whether provided directly by the company or contracted out. Patients and carers are increasingly seeking information from multiple sources, including companies. Members of the public may contact a company in writing or by telephone and request information relating to a medical condition and its treatment, most likely requesting information on a company medicine. A response can be made subject to a number of conditions.

The Code says that requests for advice on personal medical matters must be refused and the enquirer recommended to consult his or her health professional. This is designed to ensure that companies do not intervene in the patient/prescriber relationship by offering advice or information that should be in the domain of the healthcare professional. Nevertheless, with the patient's consent, information could still be provided to their health professional who could pass it on if he/she considered it appropriate.

If the request for information does not concern 'advice on personal medical matters', there is more freedom to answer enquiries from a member of the public. However, the response must be limited to that information necessary to respond to the request. Providing information that supports the proper use of medicines and enhances patient welfare is acceptable under the Code. For example it would be appropriate to provide emergency factual information on actions in the event of an overdose or to respond to a question about whether a medicine contained sugar or an ingredient to which the patient was hypersensitive. Questions about possible interactions with alcohol or whether the medicine should be taken before or after a meal can also be answered.

Learning from a Case: Auth 2098/2/08 – Corporate advertisement and associated article
A corporate advertisement in a lay magazine was associated with an independently written article that described the company's breast cancer treatments and was based on company press material. The company did not review the article. It was ruled to be an advertisement for prescription products.
Learning Point:
- Where purchase of advertising space is associated with independently written material you should ask to review and approve the article.

However, answering other types of questions, e.g. about possible side effects or off-label uses, could be fraught with difficulties and the enquirer should be directed to their HCP (although an SPC may legitimately be supplied).

Hints & Tips
When approving Information for Patients activities consider both the content and the method of distribution.

Medical information personnel should always remember that they do not have full information about the patient and their condition and are not in a position to replace advice from the patient's healthcare professional or patient organisations. This applies even if a doctor or pharmacist working for the company answers the enquiry.

Help lines, e-mail responses, etc. provided in connection with a disease awareness campaign should not provide information on a specific medicine. This is likely to be seen as promotion.

Particular care must be taken in responding to approaches from the media (Refer to **Chapter 4: Public Relations**). An SPC and Patient Information Leaflet and beyond this factual, balanced answers to specific questions would be acceptable.

As well as considering the Code of Practice, companies may also wish to consider the possible legal liability connected with advice given. Companies may decide to institute quality assurance and control processes around their medical information services.

Do not use a medical information response to promote a prescription-only product, for example, the reply should not encourage the enquirer to request a prescription for a specific medicine. Of course, each situation will be judged on its merits if a Code complaint is made.

Reference information
Reference information is intended to provide a comprehensive up-to-date library resource on a company's licensed medicine. It may be made available on a website or by way of a link from a website or by some other means, e.g. in a printed form for enquirers who do not have internet access. Companies are not obliged to provide reference information but it is good practice to do so. Providing reference information for all company medicines lends support to the

Learning from a Case: Auth 2135/6/08 – Corporate advertisement encouraged request for POM
An advertisement in the Economist headed 'Fighting Multiple Sclerosis' stated that in the fight against multiple sclerosis, the company concerned had brought to market the first therapy with long-term efficacy in significantly reducing the frequency of periods of exacerbation. It also stated that the company was continuing to investigate new therapies to give patients the most precious gift possible: a life full of hope for the future. The panel ruled that the advertisement contained statements which would encourage patients to ask their doctor to prescribe the company's product. Also the mention of giving patients 'a life full of hope' raised unfounded hopes of successful treatment given that MS was an incurable disease. Breaches of the Code were ruled.
Learning Point:
•   Ensure that corporate advertisements do not encourage patients to ask their doctor for a particular medicine.

pharmaceutical industry's position that companies are important providers of non-promotional information on medicines for patients, carers and the general public.

Reference information should include, as a minimum, the Summary of Product Characteristics (SPC), the package information leaflet (PIL) and the public assessment report (PAR) if one exists. Information based on the SPC may be presented in a more user-friendly format. Utilising the layout and linking possibilities of the internet can aid the user experience, as can including audio-visual content on websites, e.g. on subjects such as inhaler-use technique.

Additional information may be included:

▶ **Studies**: Whether or not used in a product's marketing authorisation application or referred to in the SPC, both published and unpublished studies can be provided. In practice it is unlikely that the full text of published studies would be included due to copyright considerations and the full clinical trial report of an unpublished study is also unlikely to be suitable for a lay reader. It seems appropriate to include summary information on trials in language that is understandable to the public. However in doing this great care will be needed to ensure that the text remains factual, balanced and non-promotional. Also the selection of studies presented must fairly reflect the whole body of evidence available for the medicine and must present the benefit/risk profile objectively; factual and non-promotional details of ongoing and completed clinical trials are required to be made public (refer to **Chapter 8: Research**);

▶ **Health technology assessments**: Material supplied to bodies such as the National Institute for Health and Care Excellence (NICE) can be included.

Review and approval of non-promotional information

Information on medicines made available to the public must be certified in advance by a company signatory. So advertisements, brochures, websites, etc. should go through a documented review and approval process just like advertising material for health professionals. The approval should also consider how the item will be used; so, for example, a brochure might be approved

> **Learning from a Case: Auth/2403/5/11 – Unbalanced information in lay press article**
> A GP complained that an article which appeared in the lay press promoted a POM to the public. Furthermore the information was not balanced and disparaged another product. The complainant also questioned the suitability and taste of the article because it featured an image of a woman which was of a sexual nature with a caption below describing the product as a 'wonder drug'.
> Although advertising POMs to the public is prohibited, it is possible to supply information either directly or indirectly, provided this is presented in a factual and balanced way. It must not raise unfounded hopes of successful treatment or be misleading with respect to the safety of the product.
> The Panel ruled a breach because omission of data in the press briefing on the side-effect profile in comparison to the competitor meant that it was not balanced. Neither the company nor its media agency provided the image of a woman or the caption, so no breach was ruled in that regard.
> **Learning Point:**
> • Complaints about articles in the press are judged on the information provided by the pharmaceutical company or its agencies to the journalists, and not on the content of the article. Press releases must be balanced and information on significant risks should be included.

specifically for distribution to health professionals as part of a package of information for possible onward transmission to patients. If the information is to be distributed by different means, e.g. being made available directly to patients, separate approval should be obtained. The company is likely to be held responsible for communications from agencies or others working on their behalf.

The one exception to this requirement for approval is responses to unsolicited enquiries from the public by medical information departments. In these circumstances the Code requires that written responses 'must be examined for compliance with the Code and regulations'. Consequently, it is good practice to have documented quality criteria and procedures for medical information provision that reflect these Code requirements and also to make clear how the required 'examination' will take place. Companies may wish to include training and regular updates on the Code, the regulations and their implications for medical information services. Regular monitoring and auditing would also be reassuring in the event that a complaint arose in this area (refer to **Chapter 3: Printed Materials**).

Working with patient organisations

The appropriateness of relationships between pharmaceutical companies and patient organisations (POs) has featured widely in the press with industry critics alleging improper influence. The ABPI Code outlines requirements for acceptable behaviour and for public reporting of support provided. Some requirements are based on the European industry code: 'EFPIA Code of practice on relationships between the pharmaceutical industry and patient organisations'.

The fundamentals

Companies can interact with POs and support their activities. As fellow professionals in healthcare with common interests, it is entirely appropriate that such interactions occur and are encouraged. The range of organisations that the term 'patient organisations' covers isn't defined in the ABPI Code but in the EFPIA Code it is defined as: '**not-for-profit organisations (including the umbrella organisations to which they belong), mainly composed of patients and/or caregivers, that represent and/or support the needs of patients and/or caregivers**'. This is a reasonable working definition for UK purposes. Organisations that support people with disabilities, carers and relatives and consumers' organisations are all included.

If a PO is not well known it is advisable to confirm that it is genuine and that it is an appropriate organisation to be associated with. It is important that the PO would not utilise a company's support for unacceptable purposes outside the agreement with them.

The Code applies the same principles relating to quality of information and hospitality/meetings arrangements as for interactions with other groups and individuals. The main thrust of the provisions specific to PO interactions concerns the transparency of the arrangements. Not only should the interactions comply with the rules and be appropriate and proper but also this should be open to public scrutiny.

A company is not allowed to require that it be the sole funder of a PO or any of its major programmes. The intent here is to ensure that a PO does not become dependent on one company – a situation that is undesirable. However there are situations when single-company sponsorship is unavoidable; for example when a group is first set up, or when there is very limited interest in the condition that the PO is concerned with, or perhaps when a single company is invited to support a small proportion of the costs of a particular programme.

In addition to the ABPI Code and the Regulations, there are other codes and guidelines that cover the relationships between companies and POs. In most cases the patient groups themselves, rather than companies, are responsible for compliance but when working with new or inexperienced POs, it may be helpful to draw their attention to these rules.

Transparency requirements

Sponsorship and support for POs must be declared. Each company must maintain a publicly-available list of POs to which it provides financial support and/or significant indirect/non-financial support. The value of all financial support must be declared regardless of the amount. Indirect and non-financial support must also, whenever possible, be allocated a value and listed. It must include a description of the support that is sufficiently complete to enable an average reader to form an understanding of the support provided. It is the value to the PO, rather than the cost to the company, that is important. Where significant non-financial support cannot be assigned a meaningful monetary value, then the published information must clearly describe the non-monetary value the organisation receives. Both core funding and unrestricted grants as well as funding for specific projects must be listed.

While it is likely to be straightforward to identify a value for indirect support that is invoiced (e.g. the services of a PR agency), it can be difficult to allocate a monetary value to support such as loaning a meeting room or providing the time of an employee. It is good practice to outline clearly the criteria that have been applied to calculate the monetary value of non-monetary support when it is disclosed.

The listing is usually made on a company website. In the unlikely event that the Company does not have a suitable website, and doesn't wish to set one up, then inclusion in an annual report is a suitable alternative. The listing can be made nationally or at a European level.

Support from an overseas headquarters for a UK-based patient organisation, or relating to an activity that takes place in the UK should be included if your company makes a UK listing. Otherwise include it in the European listing if you make only a single European level declaration. You can include a description of the international arrangements to avoid ambiguity or double counting when more than one country is involved.

Hints & Tips
Patient organisations may wish to make their own transparency listing available. This does not negate the responsibility of companies also making a public declaration.

Table 14: Information for patients – checklist

ASPECT	CHECKED ✓	COMMENTS
Is the communication non-promotional? Is it likely to result in a member of the public requesting the company's medicine?		
Would an independent observer judge the intent of the activity or communication as increasing product usage?		
Is it misleading, e.g. raising unfounded hopes of treatment success?		
If the information is for patients who have been prescribed the company's medicine is access reliably controlled?		
Is the information factually accurate?		
Is the information consistent with the SPC/PIL?		
Is the information balanced – as if an independent author had written it?		
Is appropriate emphasis placed on contraindications, precautions and side effects?		
Does it LOOK like promotion? Is the style of presentation appropriate?		
Is sober and understandable language used?		
Is the intended audience clear, e.g. the general public v. patients prescribed the medicine? Is distribution appropriate to that audience?		
Will the communication reach beyond the UK; or has it come from outside the UK? Check against all applicable codes and regulations.		
Are all medicines mentioned treated fairly and equally?		

Companies should establish clear procedures to capture all relevant financial and non-financial support. The list of organisations being provided with support during a calendar year must be disclosed annually within six months of the year end. A continuously updated database is an obvious way to do this. Refer to Table 2: **Summary of requirements when disclosing transfers of value to patient organisations.**

Written agreements and contracts with patient organisations

A written agreement (or several if this is easier) is required with every PO with which a company has a relationship. This must set out exactly what has been agreed in relation to every significant activity or ongoing relationship including core funding. Note that it is unnecessary for this agreement to be made public although some companies may wish to do this as part of the listing required by the 'transparency' clause. The written agreement **must be certified** by a nominated signatory.

The Code sets out elements that must be included in the written agreement:

- ▶ The name of the activity;
- ▶ The names of the organisations involved (pharmaceutical company, patient organisations and any third parties which will be brought in to help);
- ▶ The type of activity (e.g. unrestricted grant, specific meeting or publication, etc.);
- ▶ The objectives;
- ▶ The respective roles of the company and the patient organisation;
- ▶ The time-frame;
- ▶ The amount of funding;
- ▶ A description of significant indirect/non-financial support (e.g. the donation of public relations agency time or free training courses);
- ▶ A statement that all parties are fully aware that sponsorship must be clearly acknowledged and apparent from the start;
- ▶ The code or codes of practice which will apply;
- ▶ The signatories to the agreement;
- ▶ The date of the agreement.

The agreement can also set out operational details or these can be included in a separate document. Documentation must be in sufficient detail so that if personnel change, the arrangements and responsibilities are clearly set out. It will be particularly important to outline who is responsible for what, e.g. who will review and approve outputs and meeting arrangements. Certification (or examination) requirements for outputs and activities (e.g. meetings held outside the UK) should be documented from the outset so there is no misunderstanding and sufficient time must be allowed for this to occur.

Contracts

The Code requires a written contract with POs when they provide services to companies, this contract for services does not require certification. These services are only allowed for the purpose of supporting healthcare or research. POs may be engaged as experts and advisors, e.g. participation in advisory board meetings or as speakers at meetings.

The written contract is similar to those which must be put in place when healthcare professionals are engaged as consultants. It must be agreed in advance of the commencement of the services and specify the type of service to be provided and the basis for payment for the service. The agreement must fulfil the following criteria:

- ▶ Identify a legitimate need for the service;
- ▶ The criteria for selecting the service must relate to this legitimate need;
- ▶ The persons responsible for selecting the services must have the necessary expertise to evaluate whether the experts or advisors chosen

> **Hints & Tips**
> Some patient organisations will have their own written agreement templates, particularly when multiple sources of funding are received. You can use their agreement text and avoid having two agreements covering the same arrangement but it must cover all the points required by the ABPI Code.

are appropriate for the need which has been identified;

▶ The extent of the service must not be more than is reasonably required to achieve the need;

▶ The contracting company must maintain records and make appropriate use of the service provided;

▶ The engagement of services must not be an inducement to recommend a particular medicine;

▶ The compensation for the services must be of a fair market value and setting up token consultancy arrangements must not be used as a means of making payments to patient organisations;

▶ As a matter of good practice companies are encouraged to include a clause in the written contracts requiring that the PO is obliged to declare that they have provided paid services to the company whenever they write or speak in public about a matter that is the subject of the agreement or any other issue relating to the company;

▶ Each company must make publicly available, at a national or European level, a list of patient organisations that it has engaged to provide significant contracted services. The company must make publically available a description of these services in sufficient detail to enable an average reader to understand the arrangement (without divulging confidential information). The total amount paid per organisation must be reported and the list of organisations engaged must be updated annually.

Information provided to patient organisations

It is important to recognise that the Code, in referring to 'patient organisations' does not create a special category. Information on health and medicines provided to POs is subject to the Code rules, and also the law, that prohibit promotion of prescription medicines to the public. The Code sets out guidance on circumstances in which the provision of information to the public, patients and carers through POs would not be considered as 'advertising'. Advertising prescription-only medicines to the public, including POs, is not permitted.

Information provided to POs should be appropriate to their requirements. Where information on prescription-only medicines is provided to POs, it will be important to make clear the purpose of that information, how it will be used and who has editorial responsibility for outputs. It could be that the information is required for their information service 'library', or to produce a particular leaflet. A company must not seek to influence the text of a PO's material in a manner favourable to its own commercial interests. However, factual inaccuracies may be corrected.

Information in anticipation of a Health Technology Assessment (e.g. NICE) can be provided to POs. It must be accurate, not misleading, non-promotional in nature and in every other way comply with the quality requirements set out in the Code.

Hints & Tips
Although the Code does permit sole sponsorship of a patient organisation or a major programme this is best avoided wherever possible.

All information provided for patients must be certified. Information for patient groups is not immune from this requirement, although information provided in response to a specific question need only be 'examined for compliance' rather than certified. (Refer to **Chapter 3: Printed Materials** and see also **Review and approval of non-promotional information** in this chapter.)

Support for patient organisation outputs and activities

Outputs may or may not require certification by the company, in their final form, depending on whether there is a meaningful opportunity to influence the content. Any outputs that the company distributes will require certification.

Support for a PO's outputs and activities does not necessarily mean adopting responsibility for all aspects of them. For example:

▶ Providing support for the technical and design aspects of a patient-group website does not imply responsibility for the content. Unless, of course, there is a reasonable expectation that the site was set up to do something unacceptable under the Code, such as promoting a prescription only product;

▶ Printing or distribution of a PO newsletter does not imply responsibility for the content, provided the company has no influence over it.

A clearly-worded agreement is important to define the company's responsibility.

POs' websites may be linked from a company's own sites, e.g. from the reference information provided. However, be cautious about linking to their sites from advertising and disease awareness campaigns. A deep link to a page referring to products could be at particular risk of being considered advertising and control over any content updates lies with the PO. Where provided, it is generally best that links from a company's site point to the home page of the organisation.

It is permissable to sponsor POs' events/meetings providing the event does not promote a prescription-only medicine or the funding is not used to pay for unacceptable activities such as business class air fares for delegates, inappropriate hospitality, etc.

Requests to fund attendance by POs' representatives at good-quality medical meetings that are open to non-medical delegates need careful consideraion. The delegate may well be exposed to advertising of prescription medicines, e.g. in the exhibition hall, and the PMCPA has cautioned that unintentional exposure of patient group representatives to promotion could result in a breach of the Code. However, sponsorship of attendance could be argued to be acceptable if

> **Key Point**
> **Certification is required:**
> - **For the written agreement**
> - **For meetings abroad***
> - **For outputs/activities that the company has a meaningful opportunity to influence**
> - **For materials that the company intends to distribute or use**
>
> *Refer to Chapter 1 : Basic Principles – Certification and examination*

the main purpose of the meeting is truly non-promotional scientific exchange and exposure to advertising material is, perhaps, rather like a lay reader seeing advertisements in a medical journal to which they subscribe. It would not be appropriate, however, to require attendance at a company-sponsored symposium or in any other way direct the delegate to information on

Hints & Tips
Choose the declaration of company involvement to reflect the arrangements. Some possibilities are:
- **Supported by an unrestricted educational grant from 'Company'**
- **Produced by 'Company' as a service to patients**
- **Produced on behalf of 'Company'**
- **Produced by XXX with the support of 'Company'**

a company's medicines. Support for meeting attendance should be for the organisation and not for individuals.

POs' logos or other proprietary material must not be used without describing the specific purpose and the way in which it will be used, and getting their written agreement.

Any involvement in the provision of information must always be made clear even when a third party (e.g. an agency working on a company's behalf) provides the information. Simply, if the company has been involved in any way with the provision of information this must be readily apparent to the recipient. The wording chosen to communicate the company involvement must be carefully chosen and must reflect the arrangements accurately. This means that a standard phrase is unlikely to be appropriate in all circumstances. In particular do not use phrases such as 'unrestricted educational grant' unless the company was truly not involved in editing or constructing the material. The declaration must appear in a prominent position so that readers notice it before starting to read the content. For a booklet or leaflet that usually means a clear and prominent place on the front page.

Table 15: Patient group interactions – checklist

ASPECT	CHECKED ✓	COMMENTS
Do the arrangements comply with every relevant part of the Code, e.g. meetings arrangements, information quality, etc?		
Has the support/sponsorship been included in the company's public listing? *Is the nature of the support clearly and accurately described?* *Is the monetary value accurately declared?*		
Is a written agreement in place? *Has it been certified?* *Does it cover all aspects of the relationship in detail?*		
Must the outputs and/or events be certified or examined? *Has this been done?*		
Do all outputs/activities carry a clear and prominent statement about the company's involvement?		

CHAPTER 6

Goods, Services & Donations

Main clauses: 17, 18, 19, 20

The aim of the Code of Practice regarding gifts, donations or any pecuniary benefit is that these should not induce the recipient healthcare professional to prescribe or supply a particular medicine. This is reiterated by the codes of ethics of the HCP's own regulatory bodies: The General Medical Council (GMC), the General Pharmaceutical Council (GPhC), and the Nursing and Midwifery Council (NMC). These code of ethics can be summarised to state that HCPs must act in their patients' best interests and ensure that their professional judgement is not influenced by commercial considerations, hospitality, gifts and other inducements. Furthermore, HCPs working for pharmaceutical companies or their agents should not offer inducements to other HCPs. Transparency is one of the key themes of the ABPI Code.

Gifts, promotional aids/reminder items

The ABPI Code does not allow the provision of branded promotional aids, gifts or reminder items to HCPs and administrative staff under any circumstances. The Code cannot be circumvented by providing items on long-term or permanent loan.

There are a few exceptions to this where appropriately documented and certified corporately branded items ARE ACCEPTABLE, these are as follows:

▶ HCPs can be provided with inexpensive items (actual and perceived value no more than £10 excluding VAT) which are to be passed on to patients as part of a formal patient-support programme. Examples of acceptable items are peak-flow meters for patients to record readings and pedometers to encourage exercise, perhaps in obese patients. These items must directly benefit patient care and MUST NOT bear the name of a medicine and/or information about a medicine unless these details are

required for the proper use of the item. They MAY bear a Company name. These items
  - MUST NOT be given to administrative staff unless they are going to be passed onto the HCP
  - MUST NOT be given out from exhibition booths/stands but they can be exhibited on the stand/booth and demonstrated. Requests can be accepted for later delivery;
► In limited circumstances, patient-support items may be made available to HCPs even though they are not for patients to keep, e.g. where the purpose is to allow the patient to gain experience in using their medicine such as inhalation devices (with no active ingredient) or devices to assist patients to self-inject;
► Notebooks, pens or pencils can be provided at company organised meetings (promotional or non-promotional) or in conference bags. The total cost or perceived value of items provided to an individual must not exceed £10, excluding VAT. Individual attendees must only receive one notebook and one pen or pencil. However these items:
  - MUST NOT bear a product name or any information about a product but MAY bear a Company name when provided at a company organised scientific meeting, congress or promotional meeting. However if they are provided in conference bags at third party organised meetings they must not include the name of the donor company, a product name or any information about a product
  - MUST NOT be given by sales representatives during a routine call
  - MUST NOT be given out from an exhibition booth.

N.B. Inexpensive memory sticks and DVDs containing Code-compliant promotional or educational material may still be provided to HCPs and other relevant decision makers, e.g. from exhibition stands, provided the following conditions are met:
  ► The capacity of memory sticks is commensurate with the amount of data to be stored;
  ► They do not bear a medicine's name but they can bear a company name. Memory sticks bearing a company name would not be viewed as disguised promotion provided the fact that the memory stick includes promotional material is made clear to the recipient, e.g. the memory stick could have 'Promotional material from [company name]' printed on it. It would also be preferable if it opened to a page making the contents and nature of the contents clear;
  ► DVDs cannot be used by the recipient to store other data.

Advertisements for prescription medicines must not appear on any item, e.g. diaries and desk pads, that the Code does not permit the pharmaceutical company to give.

Competitions
Competitions and quizzes are not considered acceptable methods of promotion. However, the following are some examples of circumstances where they may be permissible and appropriate:
  ► Quizzes at promotional meetings which form part of the meeting's formal

proceedings and are intended to gauge attendees' knowledge of the subject are allowed but these must be:

- – Non-promotional and not connected in any way to an exhibition stand
- – A *bona fide* test of skill
- – NO prizes must be offered;

▶ Quizzes after educational meetings that are non-promotional and test the knowledge gained from the meeting are acceptable as 'educational tools'. Prizes must not be given;

▶ Competitions for patients where the prizes are health related and are given to a clinic or similar institution. Prizes MUST NOT be given to individuals;

▶ Competitions for the best piece of academic or research work, e.g. the best essay or most innovative research proposal, are acceptable and winners may be offered a grant or sponsorship or medical educational goods or services but these must not benefit an individual;

▶ In-house competitions which only company staff are allowed to enter are usually permissible. However, if sales staff participate and the competition is about a product or promoting a product, these must be approved and certified in the same way as training and briefing materials. Refer to **Chapter 9: Sales Representatives.**

Medical educational goods and services (MEGS)

Medical educational goods and services (MEGS) which enhance patient care or benefit the NHS and maintain patient care are allowed. They must not be provided to individuals for their personal benefit. The requirements of the Code cannot be circumvented by providing HCPs or practices with items on long term or permanent loan.

The restrictions regarding cost (actual and perceived value no more than £10 excluding VAT) that applies to patient support items does not apply to goods and services provided they are non-promotional and do not have conditions attached to them. MEGS can bear a corporate name but not a brand name or product trademark.

The requirement that MEGS must not bear the name of a medicine does not apply to independently-produced textbooks or journals, which include the name of the medicine in their text. 'Independently-produced' means that the pharmaceutical company had not had any input into the journal or book and which will, therefore, usually have an ISSN or ISBN. In order to prevent the provision of MEGS being, or being seen to be, an inducement to prescribe, the involvement of sales representatives must be strictly controlled. Refer to **Table 16: Key issues when supplying medical and educational goods and services.**

> **Hints & Tips**
> MEGS cannot bear the name of any medicine but they can bear a corporate name.

Table 16: Key issues when supplying medical educational goods and services

CHECKLIST	KEY ISSUES
Does the goods/service benefit patient or NHS?	*Goods/services must not personally benefit an individual recipient, e.g. an HCP.*
Could the goods or service be considered promotional?	*They must not* • *Bear a name or trademark of a product* • *Be used promotionally* • *Be used to gain an interview* • *Be referred to in promotional material* • *Be discussed in detail during a sales call*
What involvement are representatives allowed?	*Representatives **MAY*** • *Deliver goods* • *Briefly introduce the service during a sales visit. If an in-depth discussion of the goods/services is required they must arrange a separate call which must be entirely non-promotional* *Representatives **MUST NOT*** • *Have any contact with patient, patient records or data*
Has a written protocol been agreed for the supply of the goods or service?	*To avoid confusion the recipient of a service should be given a written protocol of the agreement, e.g. a GP allowing a sponsored nurse access to patient records should be informed in writing of any data to be collected and the exact use to which those data will be put.*
Is the sponsor clearly identified?	*The sponsor must be clearly named in the protocol.*
Have the materials relating to the MEGS been approved and certified?	*All materials require certification e.g.* • *Internal and external communications/instructions* • *The protocol/agreement with the recipient* • *All materials associated with the goods/service*
Confirm compliance of related materials..	*All the materials related to the goods/services must* • *Be non-promotional in style* • *Be non-promotional in content* • *Clearly identify the sponsor*
Ensure all relevant stakeholders are informed of the start date and withdrawal date of the goods/services.	*This is important as it may affect budgets.*
Transfers of Value associated with the MEG.	*Ensure these are disclosed.*

> **Key Point**
> Textbooks can be provided as MEGS BUT MUST NOT be given to individuals.

The range of goods and services covered by this clause is very wide and includes:

▶ Medical equipment;
▶ Staff;
▶ Clinical audits;
▶ Training programmes;
▶ Textbooks and e-learning tools.

> **Hints & Tips**
> MEGS must not personally benefit an individual recipient, e.g. an HCP, otherwise it will be seen as an inducement to prescribe.

In order to avoid confusion a written protocol of the agreement to provide MEGS must be drawn up. This should clearly name the sponsor, the goods or services to be provided and any access to patient data that may be required and exact use to which those data will be put. **N.B.** Transfers of value in relation to MEGS must be disclosed.

Hints & Tips
Declaration of sponsorship must be prominent and appear in all papers relating to the meeting.

All materials relating to the provision of MEGS, e.g. internal and external instructions, the written protocol and materials relating to therapy reviews, must be certified as required by Clause 14.3.

Donations, grants and benefits to healthcare organisations

This section only relates to 'donations, grants and benefits in kind' to healthcare organisations (HCOs) that are comprised of health professionals and/or that provide healthcare or conduct research. For example, a donation to a local choir would not be covered.

Company donations and awards are covered by the Code including:
- ▶ When they are made by the company and not linked to a product or any promotional activity;
- ▶ When they are made to patient organisations;
- ▶ When they are dependent on the action of a health professional, e.g. completing a questionnaire while attending a booth at a congress, this is permissible provided the donation is to a recognised charity, not in any way an inducement to prescribe and 'modest' (however, the amount is not defined).

Any donation that is dependent upon the actions of an HCP must not place undue pressure on that HCP to fulfil the actions or any other conditions for that matter.

One type of benefit in kind may be sponsorship of meetings or materials for institutions, organisations or associations comprised of HCPs or patient organisations. This sponsorship must be declared in a prominent position so that the reader is aware of it from the outset; the declaration must accurately reflect the nature of the company's involvement. Failure to do this may result in the sponsorship being viewed as an 'inducement to prescribe' or 'disguised promotion'. Sponsorship of individual HCPs, e.g. to attend a meeting, is dealt with separately in this chapter under Sponsorship of HCPs.

The following are examples of sponsorship that may be considered permissible:
- ▶ Attendance at meetings and congresses, e.g. national and international congresses organised by third parties;
- ▶ Printing of materials;
- ▶ Payment of postage or distribution costs;
- ▶ Payment for photocopying or doing it 'in house';
- ▶ Provision of finance, e.g. to support an educational meeting.

Table 17: Key issues to check when sponsoring materials

CHECKLIST	KEY ISSUES
Is the sponsorship declared prominently? [Clauses 9.10 and 19.3]	*The material must have the sponsorship declared at the beginning rather than in a footnote at the end where it may be more likely to be missed.*
Is declared on all materials?	*All materials including educational materials must bear a sponsorship declaration, even if the recipient requests otherwise.*
Has your company had 'input' into the material?	*If so the declaration of sponsorship must accurately reflect the nature of the company's involvement.*

Transfers of value and disclosure

Pharmaceutical companies must make publicly available information regarding any donations, grants or benefits in kind made each year to HCOs. Refer to **Table 1: Summary of requirements when disclosing transfers of value to HCPs and HCOs** for further information.

Sponsorship of HCP's meeting attendance

Companies may sponsor further education for an HCP, e.g. pay for attendance at national and international congresses, which can include registration fees, travel and accommodation. Companies must make the financial details of sponsorship of UK health professionals and other relevant decision makers publicly available. Further details are provided in **Table 1: Summary of requirements when disclosing transfers of value to HCPs and HCOs**.

Switch and therapy review programmes

It is acceptable for a pharmaceutical company to promote a simple switch from one product to another. However they are NOT allowed to fund services to assist an HCP in implementing a switch, where the purpose is simply to change a patient's medicine to another, without any clinical assessment. Companies are allowed to fund therapeutic reviews where the aim is to ensure patients receive optimal treatment following a clinical assessment.

Patients must be aware of the involvement of a pharmaceutical company in therapy reviews. Any patient materials must accurately declare this sponsorship.

A genuine therapeutic review should include:

▶ A comprehensive range of relevant treatment choices including non-medical;
▶ The choice of medical treatment which should not be limited to the products of the company sponsoring the review;
▶ The arrangements for the review which

Hints & Tips
Ensure that the declaration of sponsorship is precise: 'Supported by an educational grant' or 'Provided as a service to medicine' both suggest the material is 'independent' and would not be appropriate if the company had had input in any way.

must enhance patient care or benefit the NHS and, at least, maintain patient care;

▶ The facility for a prescriber to decide on any treatment change, on an individual patient-by-patient basis;

▶ A process ensuring that every decision to change an individual patient's treatment is documented with evidence to support the change.

Patient confidentiality and compliance with data protection legislation must be maintained at all times.

Joint working

The underlying principle for joint working between the NHS and the pharmaceutical industry is that the arrangements benefit patients, although it is expected that the arrangements will also benefit the parties to the agreement. One or more pharmaceutical companies and the NHS pool skills, experience and/or resources for the joint development and implementation of patient-centred projects and share a commitment to successful delivery.

When considering entering into a joint working agreement, a pharmaceutical company must take care that the arrangements do not in any way constitute an inducement to prescribe, supply, recommend, buy or sell a product.

It is acceptable to approve or decline joint working projects on the basis of the commercial value to the company. It is also acceptable to offer proactively joint working projects to those areas where the company will secure a return on investment (ROI). Companies should always consider the guidance issued by the ABPI and the Department of Health (DoH). The DoH best practice guidance and toolkit are available on its website (www.dh.gov.uk). The purpose of this toolkit is to provide the necessary information and easy access to the tools which will help to enter into joint working. The parties must have a written agreement.

The written agreement must cover the following points:

▶ The name of the joint working project
  – the parties to the agreement
  – the date
  – the term of the agreement;
▶ The expected benefits for
  – patients (patient benefits should always be stated first and patient outcomes should be measured)
  – the NHS
  – the pharmaceutical company;
▶ An outline of the financial arrangements;
▶ The roles and responsibilities of
  – the NHS and

- the pharmaceutical company and how the success of the project will be measured, when and by whom; all aspects of input should be included;
► The planned publication of any data or outcomes;
► If a pharmaceutical company enters into a joint working agreement on the basis that its product is already included in an appropriate place on the local formulary, a clear reference to this should be included so all parties are clear as to what has been agreed;
► Contingency arrangements to cover possible unforeseen circumstances such as changes to summaries of product characteristics and updated clinical guidance; agreements should include a dispute resolution clause and disengagement/exit criteria including an acknowledgement by the parties that the project might need to be amended or stopped if a breach of the Code is ruled;
► For projects started or ongoing on, or after, 1st May 2011, publication by the company of an executive summary of the joint working agreement, for example on a clearly defined website or section of a website. The NHS organisation should also be encouraged to publish these.

The Code requires the final documents for any joint working project to be certified in the normal manner. The materials used during the development of the project should be of the same high standard as the final documents but they do not need certification. The joint working agreement does not need to be certified.

Disclosure
Transfers of value made by companies in connection with joint working must be publicly disclosed. For further information refer to **Chapter 1: Basic Principles – Transfers of value and disclosures.**

It is advisable to consider the following:
► Where joint working projects involve more than one company, take legal advice to ensure that considerations in respect of competition law are taken into account;
► Consider any briefings that may be necessary, e.g. to sales representatives and other company personnel in areas where joint working projects are underway, to ensure

---

Learning from a Case: Auth 2722/7/14 – Therapeutic review
A complainant alleged a therapy review service was promotional. The Panel ruled that representative briefing material could lead the sales force to believe that signing up practices to the review was a way to achieve sales targets. Additionally, promotional material relating to 'switching' patients to the company products, while not unacceptable in itself, could be left with HCPs along with material about the review service, thus the review service could become a switching service which is unacceptable.
Learning Points:
- Briefing materials for Therapy Review Programmes must be clear and not ambiguous.
- Therapy Review Programmes must be non-promotional.
- Switching programmes are prohibited.
- Do not leave promotional switching leavepieces with Therapy Review Programme leaflets as this might then be interpreted as a switching programme.

that the joint working agreement is not infringed;

▶ All events and materials generated during joint working must be in accordance with the principles of the Code and certified accordingly.

Trade arrangements

Trade practices relating to prices, margins, discounts and free goods are outside the scope of the Code. However, schemes which enable HCPs to obtain personal benefits are unacceptable, e.g. gift vouchers, even if these are an alternative to financial discounts.

Package deals are commercial agreements where the purchase of a medicine receives an associated benefit, e.g. apparatus for administration, the provision of training on its use or a nurse to administer it, is allowed provided the transaction is fair and reasonable. The associated benefit must be relevant to the medicine involved, e.g. a spacer device with an inhaler for asthma or a nurse to administer a vaccine. However when a company employs a health professional or a healthcare organisation to provide this type of service then payments must be disclosed as a ToV. Companies are allowed to include genetic testing as a package deal where the medicine requires genetic testing prior to prescribing, even when the test outcome does not support the use of the medicine in some cases.

Samples

Samples must not be provided as an inducement to prescribe, supply, administer, recommend, buy or sell a medicine. A sample is a small supply of a medicine given to HCPs so that they can familiarise themselves with it and gain experience in dealing with it. It can only be provided to HCPs qualified to prescribe the product. They must not be supplied to members of the public or administrative staff.

The following are NOT samples:

▶ Titration packs;
▶ Free goods;
▶ Bonus stock;
▶ Starter packs.

> **Learning from a Case: 2358/9/10 – Impression given by journal advert**
> A complaint was made about a journal advert which it was alleged may give some readers the impression that all of the nurse advisors in the team mentioned in it were specialist Parkinson's Disease nurses, which was not the case. The advertisement was misleading in that regard and the Panel ruled a breach of Clause 7.2 of the Code. High standards had not been maintained and a breach of clause 9.1 was also ruled.
> The Summary of Services booklet produced by the pharmaceutical company stated that the programme advertised was non-promotional and offered as a service to medicine. The service was linked to the use of a product such that the Panel considered that it was, in effect, offered as a package deal. This is allowed provided they are not inducements to prescribe supply, administer, recommend, buy or sell the product. There was no information to suggest that the package of care offered by the pharmaceutical company was an inducement and the panel ruled no breach in this regard.
> **Learning Point:**
> • Consider the impression given as well as the actual words used in any materials.

A 'new' product for the purpose of this clause regarding samples is a product for which a new marketing authorisation has been granted, either

Hints & Tips
Samples of a particular medicine are only allowed for a maximum of 2 years after the individual HCP first requests it.

- ▶ Following the initial application;
- ▶ Following a Marketing Authorisation for a new indication that includes new strengths and/or dosage forms.

The following DO NOT count as a 'new' product with respect to sample provision.

- ▶ The extension of a marketing authorisation to include new strengths and/or dosages for existing indications;
- ▶ Additional pack sizes.

Conditions for supplying samples

The following apply when providing samples for new products:

- ▶ No more than 4 samples of a product can be supplied to an individual HCP per year;
- ▶ Samples may only be provided to a HCP for 2 years after the individual HCP first requests a sample of a particular new medicine;
- ▶ Samples must not be provided as an inducement to prescribe, supply, administer, recommend, buy or sell a medicine;
- ▶ They must not be given for the sole purpose of treating patients;
- ▶ They can only be provided in response to written requests which have been signed and dated;
- ▶ They must be marked 'free medical sample - not for resale';
- ▶ They must be accompanied by a copy of the SPC;
- ▶ The smallest pack available on the UK market must be supplied;
- ▶ Samples of medicines containing substances listed in schedules I, II or IV of the narcotic drugs convention or in schedules I - IV of the psychotropic substances convention cannot be supplied.

Control, accountability and storage of samples

Adequate systems must exist for controlling, accounting, distributing and storing samples. This should include:

- ▶ Records of number of samples supplied to each HCP;
- ▶ Records of delivery to representatives;
- ▶ Correct storage conditions:
  - – They must be stored and distributed at the correct temperature, as per the product licence
  - – They must be stored securely

  Therefore for both of the above reasons they must not be stored in a car;
- ▶ There must be audits of stock, e.g. to ensure that all stock is accounted for and expiry dates have not been exceeded;
- ▶ There must be a mechanism for return of the samples to the company.

Delivery of samples

The following requirements must be met:

- ▶ If distributed by sales representatives, samples must either be handed directly to the HCP requesting them or to a person authorised to receive them on behalf of the HCP;
- ▶ Packages delivered by post must be childproof;
- ▶ Supply in hospitals must comply with individual hospital protocols.

Outcome or risk sharing agreements

In order to get a product onto a formulary, pharmaceutical companies sometimes enter into 'outcome or risk sharing' agreements. A full or partial refund of the cost of a medicine is made if the therapeutic effect of the medicine in a patient fails to meet expectations. This is acceptable under the Code provided the criterion for when a refund or recompense is due is clearly set out in advance in an agreement. This refund or recompense can only go to a health authority, trust or similar organisation and never to an individual HCP or practice.

Patient access schemes

New drugs and treatments are assessed by the National Institute for Health and Care Excellence (NICE) to decide whether they represent good value for the NHS. NICE looks at evidence on how well the treatment works compared with available alternatives, and the cost of treatment. Drugs or treatments that are expensive and do not have a significant benefit over existing treatments are unlikely to be approved by NICE for use in the NHS.

In these instances pharmaceutical companies sometimes propose 'patient access schemes' to enable patients to gain access to high costs drugs. The Patient Access Scheme Liaison Unit (PASLU) has been set up by NICE to advise on the feasibility of patient access scheme proposals from manufacturers and sponsors. PASLU looks at the proposal made by the manufacturer to see if it is a scheme that would work in the NHS. The Pharmaceutical Price Regulation Scheme makes provisions for manufacturers and sponsors to submit proposals for patient access schemes to the Department of Health. Schemes approved by the DoH (with input from NICE) involve innovative pricing agreements designed to improve cost effectiveness and facilitate patient access to specific drugs or other technologies. This type of agreement is acceptable in principle under the Code, provided the agreements conform to its requirements. Corresponding arrangements apply in devolved countries.

CHAPTER 7

Digital Media

Main clause: 1, 4, 15, 28

The basic principles and requirements for promotional compliance which apply to other communication media, e.g. printed promotional materials, also apply to electronic media. See Table 7: Checklist of key issues when producing printed promotional materials page 54.

The PMCPA has issued guidance on digital media including social media explaining how the ABPI Code might be interpreted. In the USA, the FDA has issued draft or final guidance on various aspects of social media including character-restricted services such as Twitter and providing off-label information on social media sites. It has also issued guidance on when apps might be considered as medical devices and this is a consideration that should be made world-wide.

Internet and company websites

Prescription-only medicines cannot by law be promoted to the general public and the MHRA Blue Guide: *Advertising and Promotion of Medicines in the UK* states 'the public should not be encouraged to access materials not intended for them'.[3]

Clause 28 of the ABPI Code covers the internet. If access to the website is not limited to healthcare professionals then the website must provide information for the public as well as the promotional material for healthcare professionals. The target audiences must be clearly identified and separated so that the public don't have to access materials intended for healthcare professionals unless they want to. In practice, the site providing information for the public may be separate from the healthcare professional site.

Hints & Tips
Make a prominent statement on the website home page stating the type and nationality of the intended audience, e.g. 'This site is intended for UK patients and carers'.

If information is supplied for the public it must comply with Clause 26.2, that is, be non-promotional, factual and balanced. It must not encourage patients to ask their healthcare professional to prescribe a particular product.

If a company decides to provide only information for HCPs then access must be restricted. If a complaint were made to the PMCPA then the company would need to demonstrate that all reasonable steps had been taken to restrict access to the website. The Code does not specify how this is to be achieved but the conventional way to do this is by password protection. The usual way for validation is via a General Medical Council number or General Pharmaceutical Council registration number. It must be clear when a user is leaving a company site or company-sponsored site.

Corporate websites can include business information for investors and others interested in the company's business. It is advisable to keep such websites separate from sites directed at the general public and those directed at healthcare professionals. Each site should clearly identify the intended audience.

An internet site is the usual way of providing 'reference information' on medicines (see **Chapter 5: Patient Information**). Websites appear across national boundaries and an important consideration is whether the site is subject to the ABPI Code. Promotional or non-promotional material which is placed on the Internet outside the UK will be regarded as coming within the scope of the Code, if:

- ▶ It was placed there by a UK company/with a UK company's authority; or
- ▶ It was placed there by an affiliate of a UK company; or
- ▶ With the authority of such a company and it makes specific reference to the availability or use of the medicine in the UK.

See **Table 18: Summary of requirements for digital media** page 119.

RSS feeds and blogs

Really Simple Syndication or Rich Site Summary (RSS) is a family of webfeed formats used to publish frequently updated works such as blog entries, news headlines, audio and video in a standardised format. An RSS document is called a 'feed', 'webfeed' or 'channel'. Webfeeds benefit publishers by letting them syndicate content quickly and automatically and benefit readers who want timely updates from a website or to aggregate feeds from many sites into one place. Many websites have RSS feeds and they can legitimately be used by companies to provide information provided this information is Code-compliant, appropriate for the recipient and the recipient has agreed to be updated in this way.

> **Hints & Tips**
> If the website is NOT password protected it must have clearly separated areas for:
> • Patients
> • Healthcare professionals
> It must be clear when a user is leaving a company site or company-sponsored site.

Newsfeeds can also be incorporated into company websites. However, the company is likely to be held responsible for the content; so, for example, if an entry promotes an unlicensed use this would breach the Code. It will be important, therefore, to put in place appropriate control mechanisms if independent newsfeeds are included in company sites.

Setting up or sponsoring a 'blog' related to a company's medicine is not recommended. If a company were to sponsor such a blog then it would need to make sure that the content contributed complied with the Code, and this could be difficult or impossible to achieve. Monitored discussion pages where the company has editorial control would be preferred. Remember that the company involvement must be made clear. Caution is also required in making changes to entries on sites such as Wikipedia. The fact that contributors have the ability to change entries should not be used as a disguised method of promotion, either by making promotional statements or minimising negative information.

Search engine optimisation

Using search engine optimisation (SEO) techniques to help ensure that a company's websites, including product websites, appear high in the search return order is unlikely in itself to breach the Code. However, if there was an accusation of promoting a prescription medicine to the public, SEO might be a relevant factor. Linking a product site with a general health/disease term might indicate an intent to promote a prescription medicine to the public.

The incorporation of metadata in sites to aid search engines to find and rank highly a particular site is likely to be judged on similar principles to SEO. So, the question will be whether the nature of the metadata was such that it seems to be designed to result in a Code breach, e.g. to take patients to a site that promotes a prescription-only medicine.

On the other hand the use of SEO/metadata to encourage patients to visit a company's non-promotional disease awareness site shouldn't result in any Code breaches.

E-mails promotional

E-mails should be carefully checked to determine whether they themselves constitute promotion, if they do then they have the same requirements as printed promotional items **Table 18: Summary of requirements for digital media** page 119. should be referred to for a summary of these requirements.

However they have additional requirements or specific issues which should be considered:
- ▶ E-mails must not be used for promotional purposes without the prior agreement of the recipient. This permission should be an 'opt-in' process i.e. the recipient actually agrees to receive the e-mail, rather than to have to request not to receive them. This agreement should be in writing and records should be retained;
- ▶ Recipients should be made fully aware of the nature of the material in terms of content, quantity and frequency. For example if they agree to receiving an e-mail

alerting them about one medicine it would not be acceptable to e-mail about a different medicine e.g. the launch of a new product;

Hints & Tips
Check all Code requirements are being met if a third party is used to provide an e-mail alert service. Companies are responsible for third-party activity.

▶ Facilities for them to unsubscribe at any time must be provided;

▶ Promotional material sent electronically, such as e-mails must not give the impression that they are non-promotional. In addition the identity of the responsible pharmaceutical company must be obvious;

▶ Companies can provide e-mail alerting services often associated with educational websites. An educational alerting service could include a news item referring to a company's medicine. If it does, and the reference is considered promotional, it must comply with all aspects of the Code including the provision of prescribing information. Additionally any site to which the e-mail links could be scrutinised for compliance with the Code;

▶ Promotional e-mails should be certified prior to distribution. A record should be kept of the distribution list;

▶ It is good practice to state clearly at the top of the e-mail the 'intended audience'. This may serve as a defence in the case of the e-mail being inappropriately forwarded;

▶ It is particularly important to be careful and check that all Code requirements are being met when entrusting the responsibility for compliance in this area to third parties, any breaches of the Code will ultimately be the responsibility of the pharmaceutical company.

E-mails non-promotional

E-mails are often used for administrative non-promotional purposes as an alternative to letters or telephone calls, in these cases there is no Code requirement to obtain prior permission.

An unsolicited enquiry received by e-mail or post which includes an e-mail address can be responded to by e-mail without specific permission, consent to do so being implied in such circumstances. There is no need to inform recipients as to how to unsubscribe to an e-mail response to an enquiry. Replies should normally only be made to the sender of the e-mail enquiry and not to anyone else who is copied into the e-mail.

Pushed communications

Companies can only actively distribute electronic promotional communications to recipients who have agreed to receive them; details should be provided on how to unsubscribe from such communications.

Social media

The PMCPA has issued guidance on the application of the Code to social media activities and on the management of adverse events and product complaints from digital media. Important principles reinforced by the guidance include:

- ▶ Several clauses of the Code are relevant and will be applied to social media activities;
- ▶ Pushed communications from companies may be judged differently from 'pull' communications where a visitor visits a 'site' (rather like visiting a library);
- ▶ The intended audience, and the audience to which the communications are in effect made, is important. The intended audience should be made clear;
- ▶ It is possible for a company to sponsor social media activity without becoming responsible for the content; but only if the relationship is truly 'arms length'. Companies should not sponsor activities that could reasonably be expected to breach the Code;
- ▶ The company's role should always be made clear;
- ▶ A company is likely to be held responsible for social media posts of its employees if they relate to the company and its products;
- ▶ For each social media proposal, obligations under regulations governing adverse reaction reporting must be met. Also remember that promotional materials must include specific wording on reporting adverse reactions;
- ▶ Social media communications must be certified before release, just as for information provided through other media.

In addition to the content of social media posts themselves, a company may well be held accountable for the content of links that it provides in those posts. How this is applied depends on the circumstances but actively communicating a link to information on an unlicensed product or use is likely to breach the code. The rationale for choosing one link rather than another should be explainable.

The Code applies not only to pharmaceutical companies but to the activities of agencies or even patient groups or HCPs who are, in effect, working on behalf of the company. So ensure you have adequate control mechanisms in place. Remember also that even if the company is not held

Learning from a Case: Auth/2576/2/13 – Social media

A complaint was made that an advertisement had been placed on the Facebook site belonging to a photographic agency who worked on the photo shoot for a global product campaign. The images used had been provided with permission from the pharmaceutical company's global headquarters but not from the UK. The photographer was based in the UK and so the matter came within the scope of the Code.

The Panel ruled that pharmaceutical companies should ensure that prescription only medicines were not advertised to the public. Since Facebook is an open access website, inclusion of a medicine advertisement is. in effect. promoting a prescription-only medicine to the public and the statements were in a public forum which potentially could encourage members of the public to request a prescription for the product. Breaches of the Code were ruled.

Learning Point:

- There is a difference between putting examples of promotional material on an advertising agency's website, in a section clearly labelled as such and putting the same on a personal Facebook site. Including medicine advertisements on Facebook in effect promotes a prescription-only medicine to the public.

responsible under the Code and/law an independent organisation or individual is prohibited by law from advertising a prescription medicine to the public or before it has a Marketing Authorisation.

Social media could be used to communicate exclusively with patients who have been prescribed a company's medicine – providing they agree to receive it. Such communications must not, of course, constitute advertising a prescription medicine but the judgement on what is and is not advertising will be affected by the fact that the communications were made only to patients known to have been prescribed the medicine. Communications to this group should support the safe and effective use of the medicine.

A medical information enquiry about a medicine received via social media, must be replied privately to the individual, just as if the enquiry was received via other media. Making the reply publicly available, e.g. through 'Frequently Asked Questions', could constitute promotion.

Placing a Summary of Product Characteristics or a package leaflet on social media where it is available for consultation would not be considered as advertising. However using social media to 'push' these documents or providing edited or amended versions could be seen as advertising.

The UK Code allows companies to provide 'reference information' that patients and the public can consult. This is likely to be provided through digital media. See **Chapter 5: Patients and General Public** for more details.

As always, an important consideration in determining whether information provided in a public forum is or is not advertising, will be whether it is likely to have the effect of encouraging a patient to ask his/her HCP for a prescription for a particular product.

Learning from a Case: Auth/2612/6/13 – Meeting tweets

A complaint was made that two tweets sent by an events company (engaged by a pharmaceutical company) promoted a prescription-only medicine to the public. The first tweet invited recipients to register for a company meeting, naming the company's product by generic name and the indication in the title. The second mentioned only where the symposium was to be held.

It was ruled that tweet 1 was a breach; it was promotional because it named a POM and referred to a potential use. Tweet 2: was not a breach because it did not mention the name of a medicine or a company. The company stated that the tweet would not have been seen by a wide audience (the events company had only 55 twitter followers) but the panel ruled this was irrelevant.

There was great concern that there was no contract, etc. which set out the role and responsibilities of the events company in relation to the materials at issue. A breach of Clause 2 was ruled.

Learning Points:

- Twitter must not be used to convey information about prescription medicines which does not meet the requirements to provide obligatory information and additionally results in promotion to the general public.
- Companies are responsible under the Code for what agencies they engage do on their behalf and they must establish a compliance infrastructure for their relationship with agencies such as contracts outlining responsibilities, approval processes, etc.

Discussion forums and blogs

Company-hosted, company-sponsored and company contributions to independent discussion forums are likely to be treated differently by the Code. When a company sponsors an on-line forum this is likely to be treated similarly to company-run forums unless there is a clear arms length arrangement in place. Where companies (or their employees or agents) contribute to a discussion forum they are likely to be held responsible for their contributions.

Company-run discussion forums or blogs should be adequately moderated. Strictly, this is likely to mean pre-vetting contributions to ensure that they do not breach the Code. In practice it may be possible to have vetting almost immediately after contributions are made with immediate deletion of non-compliant contributions – but this has not been tested by a Code case. The vetting/moderation policy of a forum should be clearly and prominently stated. The intended participants (HCPs or the public) should be clearly and prominently stated, as should their nationality (i.e. British) if that isn't otherwise obvious.

Twitter

Twitter is unlikely to be a suitable medium for displaying information about prescription medicines. Its wide, uncontrolled audience means that communications are difficult to direct solely to health professionals. Even if this were possible, advertising must be accompanied by the prescribing information and other required information and this would not be possible due to limitations on size of postings.

Using Twitter to alert HCPs about some aspect of a medicine such as the publication of a new study is likely to be classed as promotion. Cases have shown that announcements on Twitter about the launch of a new product are considered as promotion and are therefore unacceptable.

Employees or others who are connected to the company should not 'tweet' on matters related to prescription products linked to the company. Clear policies should be put in place (and effectively communicated) about employees' use of social media with respect to company related matters.

Facebook

Facebook is unlikely to be a suitable medium for posting product-related information. Even if information is initially visible only to viewers who could receive it without breaching the Code (e.g. verified HCPs who have requested it, business journalists or patients who are receiving a particular medicine) the information could be easily re-posted and widely distributed. In fact, Facebook is designed to facilitate this through 'likes' and re-posts. Companies and medicines may have their own Facebook page and contributions from companies to these would be subject to similar considerations as contributions to Wikipedia (see below).

Many employees will have Facebook profiles and may well be highly active in posting information about their daily life – including work. Company policies should make it clear that employees (also agencies and their employees who are working for the company) should not comment on product related matters.

Webcasting and podcasting

A webcast is a media file distributed over the internet using streaming media technology. As a broadcast may either be live or recorded, similarly, a webcast may either be distributed live or recorded. Essentially, webcasting is broadcasting over the internet. A podcast is a series of digital-media files which are distributed over the internet using syndication feeds for playback on portable media players and computers. The term 'podcast', like broadcast, can refer either to the series of content itself or to the method by which it is syndicated; the latter is also called podcasting. Webcasts and podcasts are sometimes used to disseminate information from meetings.

If the meeting is company-sponsored, care must be taken that the meeting complies with Clause 22 (refer to **Chapter 2: Meetings and Congresses**). The company would also need to consider how the webcast or podcast was used and ensure compliance with the Code.

Wikipedia

Companies should develop standards and procedures that govern contributions by them or their employees and agents to Wikipedia and similar sites. This should cover input to monographs for new medicines and whether they will contribute amendments to existing content and in what circumstances, e.g. to correct factual inaccuracies only or to provide an alternative commentary. A company's involvement with proposed changes should always be transparent.

The PMCPA guidance acknowledges that this is a difficult area but suggests that linking to the summary of product characteristics, package leaflet or online reference information would be OK while pointing to a particular section might be less acceptable. However the nature of Wikipedia means that companies are unlikely to have much control over the monograph except to suggest additions, deletions, etc. The guidance suggests that if a company corrects certain statements it might be beholden to correct everything including competitor information. However this is untested and in the meanwhile companies should work with their medical, scientific and compliance advisors to develop standards and procedures appropriate to their situation.

Table 18: Summary of requirements for digital media

	CONTENT	OBLIGATORY INFORMATION	SPECIFIC REQUIREMENTS
PROMOTIONAL WEBSITE	In principle the requirements for printed promotional items apply so consider all items in Table 7 page 54. Approve as a stand-alone item. When certifying dynamic content ensure the content meets the requirement of the Code as a standalone item. However, the final form of digital material might not be static, consideration needs to be given to the context in which it appears but each possible combination does not need to be certified. N.B. Promotion of POMs to the public is illegal.	Promotional material on websites requires the following: • Non-proprietary name – ensure correct size and position† • Date • Reference number • Prescribing information** by inclusion in the promotional material or by way of a clear and prominent direct single click link. • Black triangle (if required). Refer to page 4 for minimum size requirements. • Adverse event reporting prominent mandatory wording*	If the website is NOT password protected it must have clearly separated areas for: • Patients • Healthcare professionals If it doesn't have separate areas it must have some means of restricting use to healthcare professionals, e.g. password protection such as GMC number. It must be clear when a user is leaving a company site or company sponsored site.
GENERAL PUBLIC WEBSITE	In UK Information must comply with Clause 26.2, that is: • Be factual • Be balanced • Not mislead regarding safety • Not raise unfounded hopes of success • Not encourage the general public to ask for prescriptions for a specific product. • When certifying dynamic content ensure the content meets the requirement of the Code both as a standalone item and within the context in which it appears.		It must be clear when a user is leaving a company site or company-sponsored site. SPCs, PILs and PARs may be placed on websites. Refer to Chapter 5: Patients and General Public.

* Mandatory wording – use exact wording: refer to page 3.
** Prescribing information: refer to page 19 for requirements.
† Non-proprietary name: refer to page 18 for requirements.

Table 18: Summary of requirements for digital media *continued*

	CONTENT	OBLIGATORY INFORMATION	SPECIFIC REQUIREMENTS
E-DETAIL AIDS	*In principle the requirements for printed promotional items apply so consider all items in Table 7 page 54.* *All the principles of promotion via mail and/or via a representative apply.*	*The following are required:* • *Non-proprietary name – ensure correct size and position†* • *Date* • *Reference number* • *Prescribing information*** • *Black triangle (if required). Refer to page 4 for minimum size requirements* • *Adverse event reporting prominent mandatory wording**	*No inducement can be offered for viewing an e-detail.* *As the material is likely to be used by representatives and viewed offline the requisite information must be provided as part of the item itself or as a link which does not require the reader to be online.*
E-MAILS	*In principle the requirements for printed promotional items apply, so consider all items in Table 7 page 54.* *All the principles of promotion via mail apply.* *It must be certified as hard copy.* *It must state the intended audience.*	*The following are required:* • *Non-proprietary name – ensure correct size and position†* • *Date* • *Reference number* • *Prescribing information*** • *Black triangle (if required). Refer to page 4 for minimum size requirements* • *Adverse event reporting prominent mandatory wording**	*E-mail must not be used for promotional purposes except with the prior agreement of the recipient. The recipient must agree to receive it rather than not opting out of receiving information via an e-mail.* *The prescribing information may be provided by:* • *Inclusion in the digital material itself, or* • *By a clear and prominent direct single click link.*

Learning from a Case: Auth/2694/1/14 – Promotion to the general public on website
A complaint was made about promotional claims for a medicine being visible on a website behind a pop-up box intended to determine whether the user was a health professional. The Panel ruled this was promotion to the public and a breach of clauses 9.1, 23.1 and 23.2 was ruled.

Learning Point:
• Make sure that the entry pop-up or screen which determines whether the viewer is a health professional does not show any material behind it, otherwise, if the material is deemed to be promotional, this will be regarded as promotion to the general public.

	CONTENT	OBLIGATORY INFORMATION	SPECIFIC REQUIREMENTS
ADVERTISING IN ELECTRONIC JOURNALS **Abbreviated advertisements are not permitted**	In principle the requirements for printed promotional items apply, so consider all items in Table 7 page 54. All the principles of advertising in printed journals apply. N.B. if the advertisement is made up of a number of screens then none of them must be false or misleading when read in isolation. MHRA recommends that each page of an electronic advertisement states that it is intended for HCPs.	The following are required: • Non-proprietary name – ensure correct size and position† • Date • Reference number • Prescribing information** by inclusion in the promotional material or by way of a clear and prominent direct single click link. • Black triangle (if required). Refer to page 4 for minimum size requirements • Adverse event reporting prominent mandatory wording*	The first part of an advertisement, e.g. a banner in an electronic journal, must include a clear and prominent statement as to where the PI can be found using a direct link. If the first part mentions the product name, the requirements of printed materials apply, i.e. non-proprietary name (refer to page 18) and black triangle (refer to page 4 for minimum size requirements). Page restriction to 2 pages does not apply to electronic journals
POWERPOINT/SLIDE PRESENTATION	In principle the requirements for printed promotional items apply, so consider all items in Table 7 page 54, especially graphs and figures that could be misleading. Include a statement on the first slide as to where PI can be found, e.g. from the sales representative, the meeting stand/booth	The following are required: • Non-proprietary name – ensure correct size and position† • Date • Reference number • Prescribing information** by inclusion in the promotional material or if being viewed online by way of a clear and prominent direct single click link. • Black triangle (if required). Refer to page 4 for minimum size requirements • Adverse event reporting prominent mandatory wording*	'Slide banks' may be used as a complete or sub-sets of slides, so that care must be taken that the presentation remains accurate and balanced. This could be achieved by having a core set that must always be presented. The slide notes/presenter notes (if any) must also be approved. If the slide presentation is to be distributed rather than presented then all the requirements of promotional materials apply and because the material will be viewed off-line the PI must be provided as part of the item itself or as a single click link that does not require the reader to be online.

* Mandatory wording – use exact wording: refer to page 3.
** Prescribing information: refer to page 19 for requirements.
† Non-proprietary name: refer to page 18 for requirements.

Table 18: Summary of requirements for digital media *continued*

	CONTENT	OBLIGATORY INFORMATION	SPECIFIC REQUIREMENTS
DVD	*In principle the requirements for printed promotional items apply, so consider all items in Table 7 page 54*	*The following are required:* • *Non-proprietary name – ensure correct size and position*[†] • *Date* • *Reference number* • *Prescribing information*[**] • *Black triangle (if required). Refer to page 4 for minimum size requirements* • *Adverse event reporting prominent mandatory wording*[*]	*In the case of audio-visual material the PI must be provided as part of the item itself or by way of a document which is made available to all persons to whom the material is shown or sent.* *They must not be able to be used by the recipient to store other data.*
AUDIO	*In principle the requirements for printed promotional items apply, so consider all items in Table 7 page 54.*	*The following are required:* • *Non-proprietary name – ensure correct size and position*[†] • *Date* • *Reference number* • *Prescribing information*[**] • *Black triangle (if required). Refer to page 4 for minimum size requirements* • *Adverse event reporting prominent mandatory wording*[*]	*The prescribing information should be in a document available to all persons to whom the material is played or sent.*
INTERACTIVE DATA SYSTEM	*In principle the requirements for printed promotional items apply, so consider all items in Table 7 page 54.*	*The following are required:* • *Non-proprietary name – ensure correct size and position*[†] • *Date* • *Reference number* • *Prescribing information*[**] • *Black triangle (if required). Refer to page 4 for minimum size requirements* • *Adverse event reporting prominent mandatory wording*[*]	*In the case of audio-visual material and interactive systems the PI must be provided as part of the item itself or or by way of a document which is made available to all persons to whom the material is shown or sent. Instructions for accessing it must be clearly displayed.*

[*] Mandatory wording – use exact wording: refer to page 3.
[**] Prescribing information: refer to page 19 for requirements.
[†] Non-proprietary name: refer to page 18 for requirements.

CHAPTER 8

Research

Main clauses: 12, 13, 23, 24

Companies must be able to show that there are legitimate reasons for all the studies that they undertake, whether they are pivotal phase III clinical research programmes, non-interventional health outcome studies or market research. There is also a variety of Code requirements, including transparency, particularly with respect to non-interventional studies.

Clinical research

Clinical research, if conducted properly and according to Good Clinical Practice (GCP) guidelines, is not considered promotional. However research that is conducted by pharmaceutical companies will usually have some impact on the commercialisation of the company's products and, therefore, care needs to be taken as to how this is organised.

It is important to ensure the following to avoid claims of disguised promotion:
- ▶ All studies must be monitored and conducted according to GCP;
- ▶ All research must be conducted with a primarily scientific or medical purpose. Ethics committee approval is a requirement and, if they are not convinced that the study meets these requirements, they may deem it to be disguised promotion and refuse approval for it to proceed;
- ▶ The study protocol (also reviewed by the ethics committee) must ensure that the research objective will be met. It must also ensure that the use of the product is justified medically and scientifically, e.g. changing patients from their current medication to the study medication must be warranted for research purposes;

► The study documentation should not be promotional in appearance or content and only refer to the product by generic name (unless the brand name is absolutely essential). Study documentation includes many items such as investigator letters, (See **Investigators** in this chapter) brochures, study protocol, case record forms and patients consent forms;

Hints & Tips
If initial letters to potential investigators contain a product name and indication, then they must be approved and meet the requirements of the Code for promotional items.

► The number of investigators and patients are necessary and justified statistically. Otherwise the study may be perceived as a 'seeding' study;
► Payments to investigators must be appropriate and represent a fair market value and since 2015 must be publically disclosed (refer to **Investigators** for more information);
► The study should be accurately and appropriately analysed, reported and submitted for publication;
► Details about the clinical trials must be made public in a non-promotional manner. The 'Joint Position on the Disclosure of Clinical Trial Information via Clinical Trial Registries and Databases and the Joint Position on the Publication of Clinical Trial Results in the Scientific Literature' is given support via the ABPI Code by the requirement that 'Companies must disclose details of clinical trials'. Further information is available at www.ifpma.org/en/ethics/clinical-trials-disclosure.html. The following are required:
  – Clinical trials must be registered within 21 days of initiation of patient enrolment
  – Disclosure of the results of completed trials for medicines which are licensed for use and commercially available in at least one country.
► Companies must provide details on their website homepage where details of their clinical trials can be found. These details must be limited to factual and non-promotional information and care must be taken that it does not constitute promotion to HCPs, other relevant decision makers or the public.

N.B. When data from company clinical trials is used in promotion, the data must have been registered registered where required in accordance with the 'Joint Position' documents.

Investigators

Consultancy agreements and payments

Payments to investigators must be appropriate and represent a fair market value for the services provided. BMA guidelines lay down rates for certain services and these can be used as a benchmark to calculate appropriate levels of payment for services provided to companies. If investigators are also practising HCPs, a written consultancy agreement is required and this agreement is the same as for other types of consultants. (See **Chapter 1: Basic Principles – Consultancy agreement**)

The requirements concerning disclosure of payments to consultants has included payments for research and development work since 2015. This includes disclosure of aggregrate amounts paid to HCPs or their HCOs related to the planning and conduct of:

- ▶ Non-clinical studies (as defined in the OECD Principles of GLP);
- ▶ Clinical trials (as defined in Directive 2001/20/EC);
- ▶ Non-interventional studies that are prospective in nature and that involve the collection of patient data from or on behalf of individual, or groups of, HCPs specifically for the study.

Costs that are subsidiary to these activities can be included in the aggregate amount.

Correspondence

Correspondence with investigators is considered by the ABPI in the same way as with other consultants, such as advisory board members. Care must be taken that the initial letter to prospective investigators does not breach the Code, e.g. by promoting products off-label. An initial exploratory letter could sometimes be considered as a promotional item, particularly if it is circulated to a large number of potential investigators. It must meet the requirements of a promotional item if it mentions a product name and indications. However once an investigator is contracted to take part in the research, letters and any off-label information will be classed as a legitimate scientific exchange of information.

Study documentation is not within the scope of the Code provided it is non-promotional in content and appearance. Other materials which do not form part of the study documentation such investigator newsletters are within the scope of the Code and must be reviewed and approved as per normal Code requirements.

Investigator meetings

Content

Investigator meetings are unambiguously covered by the Code with respect to hospitality, venues, etc. even though, if they are conducted correctly, they are non-promotional. The Code permits pharmaceutical companies to provide relevant information about unlicensed medicines under the terms of 'legitimate exchange of scientific information.' This means that the presentation of information and data concerning the methods, results and safety information from clinical studies to their investigators is allowed and this does not fall within the scope of the Code. However, this legitimate exchange would not include presentations of a commercial nature such as marketing plans, key messages or claims which would come within the scope of the Code and must comply with it.

Hospitality, travel and accommodation

The requirements in relation to hospitality, travel and accommodation are the same as those which apply to other non-promotional meetings e.g. advisory boards. (Refer to **Chapter 2: Meetings and Congresses – Advisory board meetings**)

Non-interventional studies

It is a requirement of the UK code that the company's scientific service should approve the study protocol and supervise the conduct of non-interventional studies. This approval and oversight of the study can be carried out by either a medical practitioner or a pharmacist registered in the UK.

Numerous rules have come into force across Europe designed to prevent companies using research as 'disguised promotion'. To classify a trial as non-interventional, it must meet all of the following criteria:

▶ Use licensed products in accordance with the terms of their licence;
▶ Patients must be assigned to a therapeutic strategy within current practice and not according to a protocol;
▶ The prescription of the medicine is clearly separated from the decision to include the patient in the study;
▶ Diagnostic or monitoring procedures, must be only those ordinarily applied to the therapeutic strategy;
▶ Epidemiological methods must be used to analyse the data.

Companies are now required to publish the summary details and results of non-interventional studies (where a UK company has been involved) in the same way that they have been obliged to for clinical trials for some years. Companies are also encouraged to apply the same principles to epidemiological studies, registries and retrospective studies. Non-interventional studies which are prospective in nature and involve the collection of patient data must comply with the following requirements:

▶ Must be conducted for a scientific purpose;
▶ Written protocols should be approved by the company's scientific service but there is no requirement for the protocol to be formally certified;
▶ In countries where ethics committees will review the protocol it should also be submitted for ethics approval;
▶ Supervision of the study by the scientific service;
▶ Written contracts with the HCPs or institutions conducting the study;
▶ Payments to investigators must be appropriate and represent a fair market value and since 2015 must be publicly disclosed (refer to **Investigators** for more information);
▶ Remuneration must be reasonable and reflect fair market value;
▶ Data protection laws.

Although the above only applies to prospective studies which involve the collection of patient data, companies are encouraged to comply with these requirements for all types of non-interventional studies, e.g. retrospective and epidemiological studies.

N.B. If at all possible, sales representatives should not be involved in non-interventional studies. However

> **Key Point**
> The company's scientific service must approve the protocol and supervise the conduct of non-interventional studies.

if this cannot be avoided they can only act in an administrative capacity which is clearly separated from any promotional activity.

Hints & Tips
A written agreement is required before market research can be undertaken.

Market research

Market research, although mentioned in the ABPI Code, is not normally considered promotional if conducted correctly. The British Healthcare Business Intelligence Association (BHBIA)[9] has produced guidelines in association with the ABPI. Care must be taken to ensure that the research and the materials used in it are non-promotional; otherwise it may be considered disguised promotion. It does not require formal certification but it should be examined to ensure that it does not breach the Code. It is permissible for the results of the market research to be used promotionally in the UK provided this promotion meets the requirements of the Code.

In order to be considered *bona fide* market research, the following must be taken into account:
  ▶ The market research must be clearly identified as such and the fact that it is sponsored by a pharmaceutical company must be clearly stated although the company does not need to be named (except to the PMCPA or MHRA if they request the name);
  ▶ There should be a valid research question to be answered;
  ▶ The number of participants must be justified by the objective, e.g it should not use four or five hundred participants if the research question could be answered with forty or fifty;
  ▶ Market research materials should not be product branded unless the research objective requires this;
  ▶ Product statements must be accurate and questions must not reinforce product claims which may encourage prescribing and are therefore disguised promotion;
  ▶ The participants in the market research should be selected for their relevance to the research objective;
  ▶ A written contract should be drawn up and payments must be disclosed as indicated in **Table 1: Summary of requirements when disclosing transfers of value to HCPs and HCOs;**
  ▶ The payment for participation must be commensurate with the time taken and also be appropriate to the normal commercial rate for the participant. The basis for this payment must be stated in the contract.

There is a requirement in the Code for a written contract or agreement in advance of the commencement of the market research. This contract must include details of the nature of the services provided and the basis for payment of the services in the same way as other consultancy agreements (See **Chapter 1: Basic Principles – Consultancy agreement**).

Table 19: Key issues when planning market research

KEY ISSUES CHECKLIST	ADVICE, HINTS AND TIPS
Contract	A written contract should be drawn up.
Fees	The payment for participation must be commensurate with the time taken and also be appropriate to the normal commercial rate for the participant. The basis for this payment must be stated in the contract.
Compliance with market research codes	For example BHBIA guidelines.
Research objectives and questions	There should be clear research objectives and questions both of which must be clearly documented. Only the questions necessary to meet the research objectives must be asked and you should ensure that these are accurate fair and balanced. Questions that may be perceived as gratuitously reinforcing marketing messages should specifically be avoided.
Sponsorship of the research	The market research must be clearly identified as such and the fact that it is sponsored by a pharmaceutical company must be clearly stated. The name of the company need not be stated.
Market research not disguised promotion	Market research materials should not be branded unless necessary, e.g. when advertising campaigns are being evaluated. In this case the branding and product names should be kept to the minimum necessary to achieve the research objective. The participants should be selected for their relevance to the research objective. The numbers of participants must be appropriate to the research objective, e.g. selecting several hundred participants when the research objective could be achieved with a tenth of the number, is likely to be perceived as promotional.

Learning from a Case: Auth/2614/6/13 – Market research
A complaint was made about market research which involved the respondents answering questions about a hypothetical new presentation of commercially available products. The products were referred to by brand name and panel considered the research questions would solicit interest in the current and future products and as such was promotional. Therefore, breaches were also ruled of missing PI, disguised promotion, payments contrary to the Code and promotion of unlicensed products.
Learning Point:
- Avoid using brand or non-proprietary names whenever possible when conducting market research.

The payments made to UK consultants taking part in market research must be made public, except when the company is not aware of the identities of those participating in the market research.

There are requirements for confidentiality laid down in the BHBIA guidelines. We therefore recommended that pharmaceutical companies require the market research agencies they employ to put these contracts in place rather than attempt direct implementation. The term consultant can refer to either an HCP or other relevant decision maker.

CHAPTER 9

Sales Representatives

Main clauses: 9, 15, 16

Company representatives

Companies are responsible for ensuring that all relevant personnel are compliant with the Code. This includes company employees in various departments including medical and commercial as well as contractors and any third parties acting on their behalf. However because of their mainly promotional role, sales representatives are a main focus of the ABPI Code. It is important to recognise that if a company employee is undertaking sales promotion activities they will be subject to the Code requirements for representatives even if they have a different job title or those activities only form part of their job. Companies are responsible for contracted representatives working on their behalf.

This section will cover the Code requirements that head office staff must be cognisant of in relation to sales representatives but is not intended to cover the details required by field-based staff themselves.

Sales representatives

The requirements of the Code with respect to sales staff and their activities fall broadly into the following categories:

- ▶ Training;
- ▶ Standards of behaviour;
- ▶ Remuneration and expenses;
- ▶ Promotional materials used by sales representatives.

Key Point
Sales representatives must have, a Summary of Product Characteristics (SPC) available to provide if requested for each medicine they promote.

Training

Sales representatives must be given adequate training and scientific knowledge about the products they promote. Training must also be included on:

Hints & Tips
Briefing material consists of both the training material and instructions on how to promote a product. Ensure that the briefing is clear or this may result in breaches of the Code.

> ► Pharmacovigilance. The reporting of adverse events or other significant information to the scientific service;
> ► The ABPI Code. Including written briefing covering:
>   – Meetings and hospitality
>   – Standards of behaviour for calls.

They may only be employed as sales representatives if they take an appropriate examination within the first year of such employment and pass it within two years. In extenuating circumstances such as prolonged illness or lack of opportunity to take the examination the Director of the PMCPA may agree to an extension to this time frame. The application should be made preferably by the company rather than the representative on a form available from the PMCPA.

To be acceptable, any examination from the ABPI or another provider must have been accredited to at least Level 3 by an external awarding body recognised by Ofqual. The examination for medical representatives must be a Diploma (at least 37 credits or equivalent learning hours). The examination for generic sales representatives (who promote primarily on the basis of price, quality and availability) must be a Certificate (at least 13 credits or equivalent learning hours).

If generic representatives change duties to become medical sales representatives they must take the ABPI medical sales representatives' examination within the first year of their change of duties, unless the Director of the ABPI has agreed to an extension of the time frame because of extenuating circumstances. However, medical sales representatives who change duties to become generic sales representatives do not need to take further examinations.

Pharmaceutical companies who use examination providers other than the ABPI must be able to demonstrate that its examinations are at least equivalent to those offered by the ABPI and that they will respond to questions from the authority. The syllabus studied should be mapped to and meet the requirements in the published ABPI standards. The assessment must be under invigilated examination conditions.

A candidate who has taken part of an examination and transfers to a new provider will have to demonstrate that the units already passed are equivalent to those of the new provider or take the whole of the new provider's examination.

Training and briefing materials

Companies have to prepare detailed briefing materials on the technical aspects of the products they promote.

Hints & Tips
Items for patient care must NOT be given to administrative staff UNLESS they are to be passed on to an HCP.

Learning from a Case: Auth/2591/3/13 – Conduct of a representative
An anonymous complaint claimed a representative requested a monthly appointment during 2013. The complainant felt harassed by this unnecessary number of meetings. The representative said that these visits were to fulfil a requirement by management to meet seven health professionals each day. The company provided a campaign briefing which stated 'As a minimum standard you should be aiming for two gold contacts per day and 5 others from your silver and bronze contact lists' and referred to seeing a 'minimum' of three per year. The instructions did not refer to the Code requirements concerning call rates. The Panel considered that instructions encouraged its sales representatives to breach the Code. A breach of clause 15.9 was ruled.
Learning Point:
- The number of calls made on a doctor each year should not exceed three on average excluding attendance at group meetings, a visit requested by the doctor etc. Targets should be realistic and not encourage representatives to breach the Code in order to meet them. Instructions to representatives concerning call rates should remind them of the Code requirements.

Additionally detailed instructions must be provided on how the product can be promoted.

This material must be approved and certified before use and available to the PMCPA and MHRA on request and can be used to adjudicate in the case of complaints, which by their nature often contain different versions of events. Training and briefing material includes the following:

- ▶ Training materials (both printed and electronic) including presentations and videos;
- ▶ Examinations and tests;
- ▶ Briefing documents, e.g. instructions on how to detail or promote a product;
- ▶ Letters or e-mails to representatives;
- ▶ Newsletters.

Risk minimisation plans and materials which have been approved by the MHRA as part of the company's pharmacovigilance obligations are exempt from the definition of promotion and can be delivered by a representative.

Other non-product-related briefing materials for sales representatives that are related to

Learning from a Case: Auth/2622/7/13 – Standards of behaviour
A complainant alleged that a representative had persuaded an NHS employee to send an invitation to a promotional webcast on diabetes to all GP practices in the area. The e-mail was signed by the representative as a 'Diabetes Specialist.'
The Panel concluded that this was disguised promotion because the invitation did not make it clear it was to attend a promotional web cast produced by a pharmaceutical company (as opposed to an independent medical education symposium). A false impression had been created that this web cast had been endorsed by the NHS. The representative had, in effect, created and distributed his own promotional material which had not been certified prior to use. High standards had not been maintained and a breach of clauses 2, 9.1, 15.2 was ruled.
Learning Point:
- Promotion must not be disguised. All promotional materials must be approved and certified via company procedures prior to use. It must be made clear to representatives that they should not create their own promotional materials, letters or invitations.

promotional activity also come within the scope of the Code, e.g. instructions on call rates, hospitality and meeting organisation.

Although materials intended for sales representatives require formal certification they do not require PI. They must include a date and reference number which aid traceability in case of complaint or flag time for recertification if they are still being used.

Representative-created materials

It is important that it is stressed during the training and briefing of sales representatives that any written materlals produced by them wlll be considered to be promotional and must be certified via the same route as other promotional materials (see **Chapter 1: Basic Principles – Certification and Examination**). Particular care must be taken with the use of e-mail (see **Telephone, E-mail or Fax use** in this chapter).

Briefing should include awareness that promotional materials can be created inadvertently and examples which have caused problems in the past are as follows:

> ▶ Writing about a product on the back of a business card;
> ▶ Illustrating a point during a presentation by writing on a flip chart;
> ▶ Making alterations to approved promotional materials by underlining sections,or highlighting sections;
> ▶ Adding a sticky-note marker;
> ▶ Taking materials produced from independent sources and using them promotionally.

Standards of behaviour

Sales representatives must behave ethically at all times and they must not provide any inducements (e.g. gifts, money or donations to charity) or subterfuge to obtain an interview with an HCP or their administrative staff.

Promotional aids cannot be provided by sales representatives. They may provide HCPs with inexpensive items (no more than £10 excluding VAT) which are to be passed on to patients and which are part of a patient support programme (refer to **Chapter 6: Goods, Services & Donations**).

Learning from a Case: Auth/2236/6/09 – Meetings and hospitality
A complaint was received that a pharmaceutical company sales representative had taken a group of doctors and nurses to dinner at a local restaurant for a 'purely social' event. The Panel noted several discrepancies between the company's account of events and the complainant's and also discrepancies between the representative's meeting logs. A judgment had to be made bearing in mind the extreme dissatisfaction usually required before a complaint was made. They also considered that the hospitality provided was out of proportion to the occasion and a breach was ruled. Finally they ruled that the representatives had not maintained a high level of ethical conduct and a further breach was ruled.
Learning Point:
* It would be a breach of the Code to hold a meeting at lunchtime and provide dinner in the evening.

Sales representatives may also deliver patient-support items offered as part of a mailing (and referred to on reply-paid cards). They MUST explain that there is no obligation to grant the representative an interview.

With respect to Medical Educational Goods and Services (MEGS) sales representatives may:
- ▶ Deliver goods;
- ▶ Briefly introduce the service during a sales visit.

If an in-depth discussion of the goods/services is required, they must arrange a separate call which must be entirely non-promotional.

Sales representatives must not have any contact with patients, patient records or data.

Hospitality and payments for meetings

Any hospitality must be approved and certified in the usual manner (refer to **Chapter 1: Basic Principles**) and must be secondary to the main purpose which must be education.

N.B. Delegates with the exception of speakers cannot be paid to attend a meeting. Additionally they cannot be reimbursed for travel costs for LOCAL meetings. Honoraria can be paid to speakers but not normally if the speaker is within their usual place of work, e.g. a GP presenting to other staff in his practice or a consultant presenting to other members of the department (Refer to **Chapter 2: Meetings and Congresses** for more information).

Calls, frequency and manner

Sales representatives must make clear who they are and which company they represent. They must not gain an interview with an HCP as a result of subterfuge or by offering inducements.

Learning from a Case: Auth 2065/11/07 – Call rates and bonus payments
Two representatives complained there was undue pressure placed upon them to achieve call rates and bonus payments were linked to the achievement of call rates and the numbers of appointments in diaries. The Panel noted that briefing material did reference the need to comply with the Code but that company materials did not define the difference between contact rates and call rates and even confused the two. The Panel accepted fully that it was for a company to decide upon its call rates and contact rates provided they complied with the Code but did not consider that it was necessarily a breach of the Code to require representatives to have targets for booking appointments. The company was found in breach of Clause 15.9 for not being clear enough in their briefing material.
Learning Point:
- Representatives' briefing must provide the definitions of contact rate and call rate in briefing document and the correct terminology should be used throughout.
- Unsolicited calls include proactive appointments and speculative visits.
- The limit of three calls is specific to each representative and each customer (it is NOT an average for each representative against all their customers or an average for all representatives against an individual customer).
- It is acceptable to set targets for booking appointments.

Hints & Tips - Is it a 'call' or a 'contact'?
A 'call' is where a representative makes an appointment or speculatively calls to see an HCP. Only 3 such calls (on average) are allowed per year under the Code. A visit requested by the doctor or other prescriber, or a visit to follow up a report of an adverse reaction, is not classed as a 'call'.
'Contact' is where a representative is in attendance at group meetings and similar events. There are no limits on 'contacts' under the Code.

Examples of inducements include:

▶ Insisting on delivering an item, e.g. patient support items to the doctor, rather than leaving them with the receptionist. However, when left with a receptionist, it must be made clear that the items are to be passed to the doctor;

▶ Provision of Medical Educational Goods (MEGS), e.g. a book for the library in return for an interview;

▶ Payment of a fee or even a donation to a charity, in return for an interview.

Sales representatives must ensure the following do not result in inconvenience for HCPs or their staff:

▶ **The frequency of their calls.** Representatives must not be given unrealistic targets which would breach the Code. On average three calls per year per prescriber should not be exceeded. However this does not include the following which are considered 'contacts' and not 'calls':

– Attendance at group meetings, e.g. audio-visual presentations

– A visit that is requested by an HCP or to answer a specific enquiry

– A visit to follow up a report of an adverse drug reaction (ADR)

Briefing material for representatives should distinguish between 'call rates' and 'contact rates' and it is advisable that it also reminds representatives about the Code

Learning from a Case: Auth/2477/2/12 – Representative briefing materials
A physician alleged that during a diabetes meeting, a representative had been unprofessional in that she disparaged a competitor's product and quoted unpublished evidence. The representative stated that the competitor product had recently failed a non-inferiority trial against the product she was promoting; consequently there was no clinical reason to prescribe it. The parties' accounts of what was said at the meeting differed and the outcome was dependent on the representative's briefing materials.
Although the company submitted that the representative did not tell those present that "there is no reason clinically why you should prescribe the competitor product", the Panel concluded that on the balance of probabilities, the representative had misleadingly implied that there was no clinical reason to prescribe the competitor product. This was based on the statement in the briefing material that their own product was the only choice when once-daily insulin was required and also from the impression given from the YouTube video (provided via a link in the briefing documents). A breach of the Code was ruled. The implication could not be substantiated and a further breach of the Code was ruled.
Learning Point:
• The language and approach used in representatives' briefings is important. They should not overstate the significance of study findings or encourage a course of action or statements from representatives that would breach the Code.

rules on this topic. A number of Code cases have originated from representatives complaining, often anonymously, about alleged company pressure to impose call rates in excess of those permitted by the Code. Company briefing material and e-mails are often cited in support of the complaint;

▶ **The timing of their calls.** These must be at a time consistent with the requirements of the HCP and the establishment;

▶ **The duration of their calls.** This must not be excessive;

▶ **The manner in which calls are made.** HCPs must always be treated with respect, e.g. advance notice of cancellation of an appointment and punctuality.

Detailing

Sales representatives must maintain a high standard of ethical conduct at all times. They must have an SPC available for each of the medicines they are promoting and provide it upon request. This requirement can be met by the provision of an electronic copy if the recipient agrees.

Sales representatives must report any information they receive about the company's products without delay to the company scientific service; this is especially important for adverse events. They should receive training and written instructions concerning this reporting.

When detailing HCPs, verbal 'presentations' are subject to the same requirements as printed and electronic materials. They must:

▶ Be consistent with the SPC;

▶ Be accurate, balanced, unambiguous and up to date;

▶ Not be misleading and be capable of substantiation;

▶ Not contain hanging comparatives, superlatives or exaggerated claims;

▶ Not disparage competitors or other HCPs;

▶ Be professional and in good taste.

Remote detailing

Permission must be obtained in advance or at the start of the contact or call if promotion is going to be carried out remotely, e.g. by telephone, web chat or other online calls. When this is arranged

Learning from a Case: Auth/2229/5/09 – Conditions attached to invitation to attend international congress
An internal e-mail was sent to company representatives with an attached invitation to an international congress. The e-mail stated that 'taking your customers ... would help protect our business and in many cases help grow it'. One representative forwarded the whole e-mail to a doctor. The panel considered that the e-mail inappropriately linked the offer of sponsorship to attend an overseas meeting with past or future prescriptions As the e-mail had been approved internally, the Panel was extremely concerned that this demonstrated a lack of awareness of the requirements of the Code by those involved.
Learning Point:
• You must not link invitations to meetings with prescribing your product.

full details must be given of the company the caller will represent, their role and the purpose of the call. All arrangements must be adhered to, e.g. if arrangements are made to discuss a specific product it would not be permissible to discuss a different product or a second product.

Telephone or e-mail use

There is no specific Code requirement to obtain permission for e-mail to be used for administrative and non-promotional purposes as an alternative to a letter or telephone call. However it makes good sense to be polite and ensure that the recipient is happy to be contacted in this way. It is reasonable to assume that if contacted via e-mail it is acceptable to respond via e-mail but if the e-mail was copied to a group of people it is best to reply only to the sender as the others have not directly consented to be contacted.

These means of communication must not be used for promotional purposes except with the prior permission of the HCP. Where permission has been given, each e-mail sent should inform the recipient how to unsubscribe from them. Specific permission is not required to respond to enquiries received by e-mail as consent is implied in these circumstances. For further information refer to **Chapter 7: Digital Media – E-mailing.**

Letters

These are usually promotional items and must therefore be approved and certified in the usual manner, particularly if they mention any product. Simple letters, e.g. confirming an appointment time, do not require certification. For further information refer to **Chapter 3: Printed Materials.**

The ABPI Code provides guidelines to companies recommending that clear instructions are provided to representatives as to whether and in what circumstances they are allowed to write letters (or prepare other written materials).

Companies often provide standard approved letters which are certified in advance, these are then individualised by adding only administrative details, e.g. name and address. However, it is important to remember that PI must be integral to the letter if a product is mentioned.

Remuneration and expenses

Remuneration
Sales staff must be paid a fixed basic salary and any bonus that is related to sales must not form an undue portion of the remuneration.

Expenses
Companies should put into place a policy for the approval of sales representative expenses. This should include audit and assessment in relation to compliance with the Code, for example to ensure that hospitality is not lavish or being used as an inducement to prescribe.

Pre-licence period

Medicines cannot be promoted prior to the granting of the marketing authorisation (licence). Sales representatives are by the very nature of their role involved in promoting medicines, and should not be involved in the pre-licensing period to communicate to HCPs information about unlicensed products or off-label indications. Further information is available in **Chapter 1: Basic Principles** regarding what is permissible in the pre-licensing period.

Medical information

Sales representatives may respond to simple medical information enquiries they receive if they have the relevant knowledge and have received appropriate training and briefing on the topic. However complex queries, those that require a written reply and queries that involve unlicensed products/uses must always be referred to the company medical information department. Medical information officers are allowed to respond to any unsolicited requests for information from healthcare professionals regarding the use of medicines. These can be:

> ► Within the terms of the licence;
> ► Off-label (licensed medicines outside of the terms of the licence);
> ► Medicines that do not have a licence.

However, the keyword is 'unsolicited' which means it must not be prompted in any way. The following are examples that are not acceptable:

> ► Sales representatives prompting the request by suggesting that an HCP contacts medical information, e.g. by highlighting an unlicensed or off-label use by mentioning or showing a clinical paper;
> ► Materials distributed that suggest the reader may request further information, e.g. reply paid cards (if this information is unlicensed or off-label);
> ► Discussions at the commercial section of a booth which prompt a request for unlicensed or off-label information.

Medical science liaison

The title of this position may vary from company to company, e.g. Medical Science Liaison (MSL), Medical Science Manager (MSM), Medical Liaison Executive (MLE), Health Economics Liason Manager (HELM). It is a role that has developed in Europe from similar roles in the USA where company employees (who may themselves have an HCP background) are employed to discuss medicines at an advanced technical level with HCPs.

However, the differences between the healthcare system in the USA and Europe means that the scope of the role is different and care must be taken that all activities of the MSL comply with the requirements of the law and the Code. The role is essentially similar to a field-based medical information role and similar rules apply. As the role is often information provision in the pre-licence period, discussions might include off-label or unlicensed uses of medicines. However, such discussions should only be in response to unsolicited enquiries.

Learning from a Case: Auth/2327/6/10 – MHRA complaint about health economic liaison managers (HELMs)
This complaint concerns HELMs but has relevance to other roles that provide advanced notification of budgetary implications of unlicensed medicines.
The advanced notification started only 10 months before anticipated marketing authorisation which might not be early enough. The role responsibilities of HELMs were in some respects similar to medical representatives and were expected to have selling skills.
Learning Point:
- Roles that provide advance notification concerning unlicensed medicines must have clear, non-promotional job descriptions and written instructions on their activities. Material they use should be certified.

This essentially means that the role must be non-promotional in all aspects:

▶ Reporting structure. The MSL should report via the medical structure rather than via the commercial part of the organisation;

▶ The job description, goals and objectives, briefings and remuneration package, including bonuses, must not be linked directly to:
  - individual sales, although it is permissible for a bonus to be linked to overall company performance OR
  - in any way be linked to sales figures or promotion either before or after launch;

▶ Training and qualifications. The MSL must have adequate qualifications for the role that they are undertaking. Any training and briefing they are given must not be 'sales orientated';

▶ They must NOT accompany, or be accompanied by, sales representatives when visiting an HCP;

▶ They must NOT be linked to promotional activity, e.g. at promotional meetings or staff promotional booths. It is, however, acceptable for MSLs to staff the medical information booths that are a separate area from the commercial part of the booth.

Dual responsibilities in a single role of promoting some medicines while providing non-promotional information (in 'MSL mode') for other medicines is difficult to sustain. Irrespective of the title a company gives to a role, acceptability will be judged on evidence of the activities undertaken. Role descriptions, briefing material, correspondence, etc. should all reflect a truly non-promotional role.

Learning from a Case: Auth/2754/5/15 – Call frequency
In this case the complainant alleged that the frequency of visits from a representative was excessive and that following a complaint the frequency actually increased. The Panel noted that the representative concerned was expected to achieve 6 contacts/day in total which, they calculated, equated to a contact rate of 2-3/ month for each customer. This was considered excessive and The Panel were also concerned that inadequate guidance was given as to how the representative should achieve this within the code.
Learning Point:
- If contact rates over and above 3 times/year are expected, these must comply with the code and the salesforce must be adequately trained as to how to achieve this whilst remaining within the code.

References

1 The Association of British Pharmaceutical Industry. *Code of Practice* 2019.

2 European Federation of Pharmaceutical Industries and Associations. *Code on Disclosures of Transfers of Value from Pharmaceutical Companies to Healthcare Professionals and Healthcare Organisations.* June 2014.

3 MHRA Blue Guide 2014 https://assets.publishing.service.gov. uk/government/uploads/system/ uploads/attachment_data/file/376398/ Blue_Guide.pdf Accessed 4th January 2019

4 Drummond MF, O'Brien B, Stoddart GL, Torrance GW. *Methods for the economic evaluation of health care programmes.* 2nd edition. Oxford University Press 1997.

5 Health Economic Glossary: www.nlm.nih. gov/nichsr/edu/healthecon/glossary.html. Accessed 4th January 2019

6 European Federation of Pharmaceutical Industries and Associations. *Code on the Promotion of Prescription-only Medicines to, and Interactions with, Healthcare Professionals.* June 2014.

7 European Federation of Pharmaceutical Industries and Associations. *Code of Practice on the Relationships between the Pharmaceutical Industry and Patient Organisations* June 2011.

8 International Federation of Pharmaceutical Manufacturers and Associations. *Code of Practice* 2019.

9 British Healthcare Business Intelligence Association guidelines. www.bhbia.org.uk. Accessed 4th January 2019

blue bold *indicates main entry in the text*
bold *indicates entry in a table*

Index